Editor
Eric Migliaccio

Editorial Project Manager
Ina Massler Levin, M.A.

Editor in Chief
Sharon Coan, M.S. Ed.

Cover Artist
Agi Palinay

Art Coordinator
Cheri Macoubrie Wilson

Creative Director
Elayne Roberts

Imaging
James Edward Grace

Product Manager
Phil Garcia

Publishers
Rachelle Cracchiolo, M.S. Ed.
Mary Dupuy Smith, M.S. Ed.

Take Five Minutes:

365

Calendar-Related Editing Activities

W9-AHT-422

Author

Bobi Thompson, M.A.

Teacher Created Materials

Teacher Created Materials, Inc.
6421 Industry Way
Westminster, CA 92683
www.teachercreated.com
ISBN-1-57690-515-2
©1999 Teacher Created Materials, Inc.
Made in U.S.A.

Table of Contents

Introduction

Beginning a class by engaging students in an activity that is easily understood, self-directed, and interesting to do, and which also imparts new information, is a challenge to even the most experienced teacher. *Take Five Minutes: 365 Calendar-Related Editing Activities* meets that challenge.

This book features sentences that need to be edited—everything from capital letters to end punctuation is left out. Students will need to check these sentences for all manner of errors (e.g., spelling, punctuation, usage, etc.) and correct them as needed. Presented in calendar order, the sentences catalog many of the important events that have occurred throughout history—from the birth dates of world leaders, scientists, entertainers, etc., to the pivotal dates behind the histories of many nations. In this way, a lesson on grammar is combined with an overview of history.

Each "day" of sentences takes approximately five minutes to complete—just the five minutes busy teachers need to take roll, collect homework, or review a project with an individual student. An answer key is provided at the end of the book, enabling the teacher to either correct the sentences with the group or individually or have the students self-check their own work. Whichever way is chosen, the key makes correcting these sentences a breeze.

While some dates will probably always "live in infamy," each of the 365 days of the year (and leap day, too!) has been the setting for at least a few noteworthy events or births. *Take Five Minutes: 365 Calendar-Related Editing Activities* supplies these bits of facts and trivia within the context of the calendar but minus the clarity of correct grammar. This book gives your students the opportunity to "rewrite" history.

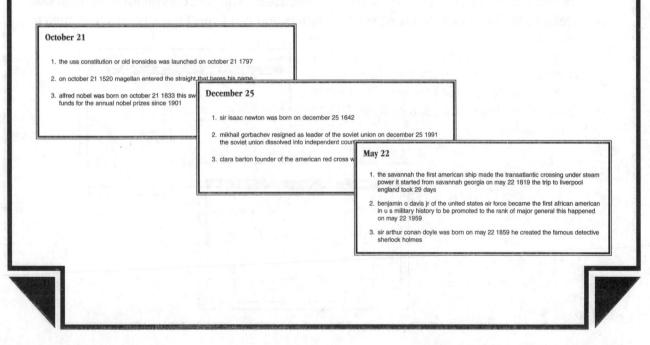

How to Use This Book

The sentences contained within *Take Five Minutes: 365 Calendar-Related Editing Activities* can be presented in a variety of ways.

- A teacher can choose to reproduce the page for each student to correct. A student can either copy the sentences correctly or correct them directly on the reproduced page.

- Since each calendar day is presented on a separate card (three per page), the pages can be reproduced onto cardstock, cut, and then put into a file box. In this way, students can work exclusively on the date(s) you have assigned. The cards can then be set up at a center. Also, a card file can be made available for students who miss their daily editing task. The answer key for each set of sentences can be reproduced and placed on the back of its corresponding card for self-correcting.

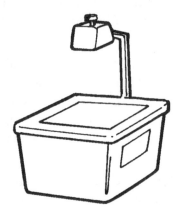

- The sentences can be copied onto an overhead transparency. This can already be projected by the overhead onto a screen when the students enter the classroom. Students will then have the opportunity to begin working immediately on their daily edit. When completed, the students' work can be reviewed either orally or in writing by the teacher or a student working at the overhead. The same exercise can be done using a chalkboard or dry-erase board. Let students use different colored markers or chalk when correcting these for the whole class.

- Depending on the grade level and the ability of the class, adjust the sentences to meet the individual needs of your students. In some cases, you will choose no more than one sentence to share with the class, while in others you can expect the students to complete them all.

- Have your students utilize the blank calendar grids provided (pages 129–134) to record their grades for each of their daily editing tasks.

Editing

Activities

There are several ways to use these sentences to both enhance your students' learning and attract their interest.

- Since these sentences are all related to calendar dates, you can choose those that correspond to the current date.
- Use the sentences as an introduction to your lesson.
- Use the sentences to review the rules of grammar and capitalization.
- To challenge your students further and test their knowledge of history, you may want to delete portions of the sentences. For instance, an entry for December 25th reads "Clara Barton, founder of the American Red Cross, was born on December 25, 1821." Here, you may want to omit either "Clara Barton" or "American Red Cross" and have your students supply the missing information. In this way, you can use the sentences as a springboard for outside research.
- Find out the birth dates of your students. When one of their birthdays falls on a day you are going to use, create a sentence which includes basic information about the birthday person. For example, you may want to create a sentence such as "Happy Birthday, Rita! Rita Juster was born on May 12, 1986, in Corona, California," and include it with the other sentences provided for May 12th. Remember to omit all of the punctuation and capitalization first, though. (Note: Make sure to keep the information about the birthday person minimal. Especially for older children, the more personal the information, the more potential for problems to arise.)

Rules of Grammar

To say that correctly punctuating the English language can be difficult would be an understatement. Perfect grammar can be a tricky business, filled with subtle nuances and intricacies. Having said that, the rewards for possessing the ability to construct clear, precise sentences are immeasurable. In all phases of life, writing is one of the most valuable forms of communication available.

Care has been taken to make the sentences in *Take Five Minutes: 365 Calendar-Related Editing Activities* age-appropriate and realistic for the abilities of your fourth through eighth grade students. The types of punctuation and usage you will find in this book are the following:

- Periods: These will be needed for both end punctuation and abbreviations.
- Question Marks: These will occasionally appear in this book.

Editing *(cont.)*

Rules of Grammar *(cont.)*

- Spelling: The sentences in this book will often contain misspelled words. Sometimes commonly misspelled words will be featured (e.g., *seperate* instead of *separate, independant* instead of *independent,* etc.). Sometimes a homophone will appear in the place of the appropriate word (e.g., *there* for *their, piece* for *peace,* etc.). At other times, the incorrect tense or form of a *to be* verb will be present.

- Capitalization: All words in the main section of this book are presented in lowercase. Students will not only need to capitalize the first letter of the first word of each sentence but also any proper nouns that occur throughout the sentence. (These include many acronyms, such as *NASA*.)

- Exclamation Points: Exclamation points are more subjective than most other forms of punctuation, and so when they appear in this book, they are more of a suggestion than a rule. Your students may use these marks more or less frequently than the answer key suggests. It is generally better to underuse exclamation points than overuse them.

- Commas: These will be needed to separate items in a series, to punctuate dates within a sentence, and to separate introductory clauses from the main body of the sentence.

- Apostrophes: Apostrophes are often used to show ownership. Also, they may be needed when letters or numbers have been omitted (e.g., '80 for 1980, rock 'n' roll).

- Quotation Marks: Some famous quotes have been added to these sentences; they will require quotation marks. Also, nicknames and titles of songs and poems need quotation marks.

- Italics/Underlining: Titles of books, movies, plays, anthologies, paintings, and sculptures need to be italicized—along with the specific names of air-, land-, sea- and spacecraft (e.g., *Apollo 8, Titanic*). (**Note:** Since it is impractical to write italics by hand, students should underline the title in question.)

- Colons: These marks are used sparingly in this book. They may be necessary to separate hours and minutes (e.g., 11:30) or to introduce a series of items.

- Semicolons and long dashes: The use of these marks is never mandatory in the sentences presented in this book. However, if a student has a grasp on how to substitute these marks for commas and periods, allow him or her to do so.

- Hyphens: In this book, hyphens are sometimes used to conjoin compound words (e.g., part-time, jack-o'-lantern, etc.).

- Parentheses: Parentheses are occasionally necessary when punctuating the sentences in this book. When information is extremely peripheral (or parenthetical), the use of parentheses is preferred over the use of commas.

- Slashes: Slashes or hyphens can be used to separate numbers in a date (e.g., 9/8/98). Also, slashes can, at times, be used in the place of a conjunction (e.g., football/baseball player, aspiring singer/dancer, etc.).

January 1

1. sudan was proclaimed a independent nation on january 1 1956 sudan is on the contenent of africa

2. the laws outlined in the amancipation proclamation went into affect on january 1 1863 it was signed by president abraham lincoln

3. great americans betsy ross flagmaker and paul revere soldier and patriot was born on this date ross was born in 1752 revere was born in 1735

4. in pasadena ca the tournament of roses has taken place on this date since 1886

January 2

1. the first commemorative postage stamp was issued by the united states post office department on january 2 1893

2. georgia became a state in 1776 it was the forth state to ratify the constitution it did so on january 2 1788 it seceded on january 19 1861 and was re admitted on july 15 1870

3. today is national science fiction day isaac asimov a famous science fiction writer was born on this day in 1920

January 3

1. alaska is the largest state in the united states it is more than twice the size of texas alaska entered the union on january 3 1959 it is our fourty nine state

2. the march of dimes was exstablished on january 3 1938 to raze funds for polio research

3. lucretia coffin mott a womans rights advocate was born on january 3 1793

4. the battle of princeton took place on january 3 1777

January 4

1. louis braille inventer of the braille alphabet system for the blind was born on this date in 1809

2. english scientist sir isaac newton discover of the law of gravity was born on january 4 1642

3. utah became the fourty fifth state on january 4 1896

4. jacob grimm author of fairy tales was born on january 4 1785

January 5

1. nellie tayloe ross became the first women govenor in the united states she became govenor of wyoming on january 5 1925

2. the great northern railway was completed on january 5 1893

3. today is bird day the national audubon society was founded in 1905

4. stephen decatur a united states naval hero was born on january 5 1779

January 6

1. new mexico become the 47 state on this day in 1912

2. carl sandburg a poet and author was born on january 6 1878

3. pan american airways achieved the first around the world commercial flight on january 6 1942

4. george washington carver was born a slave on january 6 1864 in diamond grove missouri

January 7

1. president milard fillmore was born on january 7 1800 he was are thirteenth president he belonged to the whig political party

2. transatlantic telephone service began on january 7 1927

3. the first national election in the united states took place on january 7 1789

4. the first united states commercial bank opened in philadelphia on january 7 1782

January 8

1. rock n roll performer elvis presley was born on january 8 1935

2. andrew jackson defeated the british at the battle of new orleans on january 8 1815

3. president washington delivered the first state of the union address on january 8 1790

January 9

1. president richard nixon our thirty seven presidant was born on january 9 1913

2. the seeing eye organization was incorporated on january 9 1929 it trains dogs to guide the blind the organization is located in morristown new jersey

3. carrie chapman catt a womans suffrage leader was born on january 9 1859

4. the first united states baloon flight happened on january 9 1793

January 10

1. ethan allen leader of the green mountain boys was born on january 10 1738

2. the first oil strike in texas happened on january 10 1901

3. the first session of the united nations took place on january 10 1946

4. the first racial integration of public education in georgia happened on january 10 1961

January 11

1. alexander hamilton the first secretary of the united states treasury was born on january 11 1757

2. on this day in 1964 u s surgeon general luther terry issued the first government warning stating that smoking may be hazardous to a persons health

3. philosopher william james was born on january 11 1842 he said that people only use 10% of their minds

January 12

1. playwright lorraine hansberry who wrote a raisin in the sun died on january 12 1965

2. fairy tail righter charles perrault was born on january 12 1628 he write sleeping beauty little red riding hood and cinderella

3. the first public museum was founded in charleston south carolina on january 12 1773

January 13

1. stephen foster died on this day in 1864 he wrote the songs oh susanna and camptown races

2. the accordion was patented on january 13 1854

3. horatio alger a novelist was born on january 13 1834

4. the first public radio broadcast took place on this day in 1910 it featured several opera singers

January 14

1. the simpsons an animated tv series premiered on january 14 1990

2. born in england on january 14 1886 hugh lofting wrote many books including his doctor doolittle series

3. albert schweitzer a humanitarian was born on january 14 1875

4. american officer benedict arnold was born on this date in 1741 he deserted to the british during the revolutionary war

January 15

1. martin luther king jr leader of the nonviolent civil rights movement in the united states in the 60s was born in alanta georgia on january 15 1929

2. the first annual super bowl was played on january 15 1967 on that day the green bay packers won the kansas city chiefs 35 10

3. mathew b brady the first photographer to record civil war battlefields died on january 15 1896

January 16

1. robert service a poet was born on january 16 1874

2. the civil service system was established on january 16 1883

3. the us national aeronautics and space administration nasa accepted its first woman candidates for astronauts on january 16 1978

January 17

1. rutherford birchard hayes are nineteen presidant died on january 17 1822 he was born in delaware ohio after retiring from the presidency he lived in fremont ohio

2. happy birthday ben benjamin franklin a scientist and statesman was born on january 17 1706

3. prizefighter muhammed ali was born on january 17 1942 in louisville kentucky his given name was cassius clay

January 18

1. daniel webster a statesman was born on january 18 1782

2. a a milne author of the winnie the pooh books was born january 18 1882

3. peter roget was born on january 18 1779 his name is synonymous with the thesaurus

January 19

1. confederate general robert e lee was born on january 19 1807

2. james watt inventer of steam power was born on this date in 1736

3. edgar allan poe was born on january 19 1809 he wrote many famous tales of horror

January 20

1. congress ratified the twenty amendment to the constitution in 1933 it stated that a presidents term of office would begin on january 20 rather then march 4

2. the main event of inauguration day the day the new president takes the oath of office occurs at noon on january 20th on the capital steps in washington d c

3. on january 20 1981 the same day that ronald reagan was inaugurated as president of the united states the iranian hostage crisis ended and 52 american captives were released

January 21

1. nautilus the first atomic powered ship was launched on january 21 1954 it was the first ship to reach the north pole it did so on august 3 1958

2. confederate general stonewall jackson was born on january 21 1824

3. the first novel published in america was published on this day in 1789

January 22

1. the first postal route which was from boston to new york was established on january 22 1672

2. andre ampere was born on january 22 1775 the ampere the unit of electrical current was named after him

3. a vietnam war peace agreement was signed on january 22 1973 it called for a cease fire throughout north and south vietnam

January 23

1. john hancock was born today in 1737 he was the first man to sign the declaration of independence

2. the us navy bathysphere trieste went 24000 feet to the bottom of mariana trench in the pacific ocean on january 23 1960

3. althea gibson became the first african american voted female athelete of the year it happened on january 23 1958

January 24

1. maria tallchief a american ballerina was born on january 24 1925

2. john sutter found gold in sacramento valley california on january 24 1848

3. on january 24 1962 jackie robinson became the first african american elected to the national baseball hall of fame

4. the first ice cream bar the eskimo pie was patented on this day in 1922

January 25

1. on january 25 1998 john elway led the denver broncos in there victory over the green bay packers the win was the broncos first in five attempts since 1978

2. the first transcontinental telephone call took place on january 25 1915 it was placed between san francisco and new york

3. on january 25 1961 president john f kennedy held the first televised presidential news conference.

January 26

1. michigan became the twenty six state on january 26 1837

2. general douglas macarthur was born on january 26 1880

3. on january 26 1961 hockey player wayne gretzky was born

4. australia the worlds only country continent was first settled by colonists on january 26 1788

January 27

1. wolfgang amadeus mozart was born on january 27 1756

2. lewis carroll charles dodgson author of alice in wonderland was born on this date in 1832

3. today is the anniversary of the official signing of a peace agreement ending the vietnam war the agreement was reached in 1973

4. three apollo 1 astronauts was killed in a fire during ground testing on january 27 1967

January 28

1. south carolina and six other states succeded from the united states on january 28 1861 they called themselfs the confederate states of america and named jefferson davis there leader

2. sir francis drake a english explorer was born on this date in 1540

3. on january 28 1986 seven astronauts was killed in the challenger explosion at the kennedy space center in florida

4. the us coast guard was established on january 28 1915

January 29

1. are twenty five president william mckinley was born on january 29 1843 in niles ohio he was assassinated by leon czolgosz he was one of our most loved presidents'

2. kansas became the thirty forth state on january 29 1861

3. thomas paine an revolutionary war patriot and writer was born on january 29 1737

January 30

1. franklin delano roosevelt was born on this date in 1882 he is the only president to be elected to for terms he was are thirty two president

2. the baseball hall of fame was established on january 30 1936

3. mahatma gandhi was assassinated on january 30 1948 gandhi didnt believe in using violence to achieve ones goals

January 31

1. the united states launched its first satelight explorer 1 on january 31 1958

2. several great major league baseball players were born on january 31 jackie robinson most known for breaking the color barrier in baseball was born on january 31 1919 also ernie banks whose nickname was mr cub was born on this date in 1931 and nolan ryan the all time strikeout king was born on january 31 1947

3. the first mcdonald's restaurant in the soviet union opened on this day in 1990

February 1

1. today is robinson crusoe day alexander selkirk the scottish sailor who became the model for daniel defoes robinson crusoe was rescued from the juan fernandez islands on febuary 1 1709

2. langston hughes a poet was born on febuary 1 1902

3. julia ward howes battle hymn of the republic was published on febuary 1 1862

February 2

1. happy ground hog day did the ground hog sea his shadow if so its six more weaks of winter

2. irish novelist james joyce was born on february 2 1882

3. on february 2 1935 the first lie detector test was taken

February 3

1. elizabeth blackwell was born on february 3 1821 in 1849 she became the first american women to recieve a degree as a medical doctor

2. norman rockwell a popular america painter was born on february 3 1884

3. the fifteen amendment to the u. s. constitution granted all citizens the right to vote and was ratified on february 3 1870

February 4

1. charles a lindbergh a aviator was born on february 4 1902 he was the first person to fly across the alantic ocean alone he becomed none as lucky lindy

2. rosa parks mother of the modern civil rights movement was born on february 4 1913

3. the confederate states of america was founded in alabama on february 4 1861

February 5

1. roger williams founder of rode island arrived in america on february 5 1631

2. hank aaron was born on february 5 1934 he becomed the all time home run king when he hit his 715 home run in 1974 he breaked the record of babe ruth

3. the longest war in history ended on february 5 1985 the third punic war began in 149 b c and lasted 2131 years

February 6

1. ronald reagan our fourty president was born on febuary 6 1911 he was the oldest man ever elected as president age 69 in 80 73 in 84

2. massachusetts became the sicks state to ratify the constitution it did so on febuary 6 1788

3. george herman babe ruth was born on febuary 6 1895 he hit 714 home runs during his career he hit many of his home runs in yankee stadium it became known as the house that ruth built

February 7

1. frederick douglass an escaped slave who became a leading abolitionist was born on february 7 1817

2. charles dickens a english novelist was born on this date in 1812

3. sinclair lewis a novelist was born on february 7 1885

4. laura ingalls wilder was born on this day in 1867 she beginned righting the little house books when she was sixty five years old

February 8

1. the boy scouts of america were founded on february 8 1910

2. on february 8 1735 the first opera in the american colonies was performed

3. writer jules verne was born on february 8 1823 twenty thousand leagues under the sea and around the world in eighty days was published in 1873 these books are still popular today

4. actor james dean was born on this day in 1931

February 9

1. the united states weather service was established on february 9 1870

2. william henry harrison are nine president was born on febuary 9 1773

3. on febuary 9 1909 the first school to give scientific training in the care and preservation of shade trees was founded

February 10

1. the first singing telegram was sent on febuary 10 1933

2. samuel plimsoll born on febuary 10 1824 was upset about the overloading of cargo ships he worked to pass laws limiting how much could be put on ships

3. olympic swimmer mark spitz was born in modesto california on febuary 10 1950 he set a world record at the 1972 olympic games in munich germany by winning seven gold metals

February 11

1. thomas alva edison was born on febuary 11 1847 edison said that genius is 1% inspiration and 99% perspiration

2. today is national inventors day

3. the first hospital in america opened in philadelphia on febuary 11 1751 benjamin franklin and dr thomas hood worked to establish this hospital

February 12

1. abraham lincoln was born on february 12 1809 he was are sixteen president we selebrate presidents day the third monday in february to honor presidant washington and presidant lincoln

2. the national association for the advancement of colored people naacp was founded on this date in 1909

3. thaddeus kosciusko a polish patriot and aide to general washington was born on february 12 1746

4. charles darwin was born in shrewsbury england on february 12 1809

February 13

1. boston latin grammer school the oldest public school still in existance in the united states began on february 13 1635

2. grant wood a american primitive painter was born on february 13 1892

3. the first magazine published in america the american magazine was presented on february 13 1741

February 14

1. arizona become the forty ate state on february 14 1912

2. oregon become the thirty three state on february 14 1859

3. today is valentines day

4. g w gale ferris was born on february 14 1859 what amusement park ride do you suppose he introduced

February 15

1. cyrus mccormick a inventor was born on febuary 15 1809

2. galileo galilei a italian astronomer and mathematician was born on this date in 1564

3. susan b anthony a crusader for womans rights was born on febuary 15 1820

4. charles tiffany born on this day in 1812 is known for his jewlry designs and jewlry store his son louis tiffany born on febuary 18 1848 is none for his intricate art work of stained glass

February 16

1. henry adams a historian was born on febuary 16 1838

2. on febuary 16 1960 the submarine triton left new london connecticut on a trip around the world it returned on may 11

3. yonge street in toronto canada is the worlds longest street it opened on febuary 16 1796

February 17

1. today is pta founders day the national congress of parents and teachers were founded on febuary 17 1897

2. the war of 1812 ended on febuary 17 1815

3. marian anderson a contralto singer was born on febuary 17 1902

4. basketball star michael jordan was born on february 17 1963

February 18

1. san franciscos golden gate international exposition opened on february 18 1939

2. clyde w tombaugh discovered are fartherest planet pluto on february 18 1930 pluto is the outermost of the nine planets in are soler system

3. mark twains the adventures of huckleberry finn was published on this day in 1885

February 19

1. thomas edison patented the phonograph on this day in 1878

2. nicolaus copernicus a astronomer of polish decent was born on february 19 1473 he founded modern astronomy around 1543 he discovered that earth is a moveing planet and the son is the center of the solar system

3. the manufacturers of cracker jacks began including a prize in each box on this day in 1913

February 20

1. on february 20 1962 leutenant colonel john glenn jr became the first american to orbit earth

2. the united states purchased the virgin islands from denmark on february 20 1917

3. today in 1872 the metropolitan museum of art opened in new york city

4. frederick douglass died on february 20 1895 he was born a slave in tuckahoe maryland he gained his freedom by escaping from his master

February 21

1. the washington monument built in honor of are first presidant was dedicated on febuary 21 1885

2. on febuary 21 1878 the first telephone directory was issued in new haven connecticut

3. on february 21 1972 richard nixon became the first u s president to visit china

February 22

1. george washington was born on this date in 1732 he was are first presidant

2. frank w woolworth opened his first 5 cent store on febuary 22 1879

3. on this day in 1924 president calvin coolidge made the first public radio broadcast from the white house

February 23

1. john quincy adams our sixth presidant and the sun of our second presidant died on this date in 1848

2. the marines raised the united states flag on mt suribachi iwo jima on febuary 23 1945 this took place after a battle during world war 2 a photographer took there picture and one a pulitzer prize

3. george frideric handel was born on febuary 23 1685 he is considered one of the greatest musicians of all time

February 24

1. pope gregory the thirteenth established the modern calender on febuary 24 1582

2. the first rocket to reach outer space blasted off from white sands proving grounds new mexico on this date in 1949 this too stage rocket reached an atitude of 250 miles

February 25

1. the income tax law was adopted on febuary 25 1913 with the passing of the sixteen amendment

2. francisco coronado embarked upon the exploration of mexico and the southwestern united states on this date in 1540

3. the first timberland protection act was passed by congress on febuary 25 1779

4. adelle davis a american nutritionist and author was born on febuary 25 1905 she message was you are what you eat

5. hiram rhodes revels was the first african american to take office as a united states senator he did so on febuary 25 1870

February 26

1. william buffalo bill cody was born on febuary 26 1846

2. the first around the world nonstop airplane flight took off from fort worth texas on febuary 26 1949

3. levi strauss was born on this date in 1829 he is the inventer of blue jeans

4. congress established the grand canyon in arizona as a national park on febuary 26 1919

February 27

1. henry wadsworth longfellow a poet was born on febuary 27 1807 won of his popular poems is called the song of hiawatha

2. voting by woman were declared legal by the supreme court on this date in 1922

3. the twenty two amendment to the constitution was ratified on this date in 1951 it stated that no person shall be elected to the office of the president more than twice

4. the gulf war ended on february 27 1991 forty days after it had beginned

February 28

1. the republican party was organized on febuary 28 1854

2. the final episode of m a s h aired on this day in 1983 this event was the most watched series tv show ever

3. vaslav nijinsky a famous ballet dancer was born on febuary 28 1890 he was born in kiev russia

February 29

1. leap year happens every four years this extra day is added to make are calender year more nearly match the soler system

2. on this day in 1940, gone with the wind won the academy award for best motion picture of 1939 one member of the films cast hattie mcdaniel became the first african american actress to win an oscar

March 1

1. ohio has become the united states seventeen state on march 1 1803 president thomas jefferson was presidant at that time it's capitol is columbus
2. nebraska became the thirty seven state on march 1 1867
3. yellowstone became the first national park in the united states on march 1 1872 it was established in idaho wyoming and montana
4. the first united states census was authorized by congress on this date in 1790 the results virginia was the most populated state and philadolphia pennsylvania was the most populated american city
5. on march 1 1780 pennsylvania became the first state to officially abolish slavery

March 2

1. wilt chamberlain a basketball star scored one hundred points against the new york knickerbockers on march 2 1962

2. theodore seuss geisel dr seuss was born on march 2 1904

3. sam houston a frontiersman was born on this date in 1793

4. today is national teachers day have you hugged your teacher today

March 3

1. florida became the twenty seven state on march 3 1845 it seceded in 1861 and was re admiteed in 1868

2. on march 3 1931 president hoover signed a bill making the star specked banner the national anthem

3. the adhesive postage stamp was first approved by congress on this date in 1847

4. alexander graham bell inventor of the telephone was born on march 3 1847

March 4

1. vermont joined the union as the fourteen state on march 4 1791

2. today is constitution day the united states constitution went into affect on march 4 1789

3. garrett morgan inventor of the gas inhaler and traffic signal was born today in 1877

4. the united states congress created the department of labor on march 4 1913 the departments purpose is to protect the welfare of workers in the united states

March 5

1. gerard mercator a flemish mapmaker was born on march 5 1512

2. the first bloodshed of the american revolution took place on this date in 1770 its known as the boston massacre

3. today is crispus attucks day on march 5 1770 this black member of a group of boston patriots was the first person to die in the boston massacre

March 6

1. on march 6 1836 the alamo was captured after holding out for nearly too weaks texans fortified in the alamo was killed by the mexican general santa ana

2. michelangelo buonarroti a italian artist was born on this date in 1475 he painted the ceiling of the sistine chapel and is considered one of the worlds gratest artists

3. the united states bureau of census was established on march 6 1902

4. ghana became a independant nation on march 6 1957

March 7

1. luther burbank a botanist and horticulturist was born on this date in 1849

2. victor farris inventer industrialist and multimillionaire died on march 7 1985 of the 200 patents he owned his best none patent is probably the paper milk carton

3. alexander graham bell patented the telephone on march 7 1876

March 8

1. the first american combat troops arrived in vietnam on march 8 1965

2. on march 8 1945 phyllis mae daley became the first african american woman to be commissioned in the navy nurse cores

3. oliver wendell holmes jr a supreme court justice was born on march 8 1841

4. today is international womens day

March 9

1. the battle between the monitor and merrimack took place on march 9 1862 it was a famous see battle during the civil war

2. amerigo vespucci was born on march 9 1454 he be a explorer

3. richard adams died today in 1988 adams invented the paint roller during world war 2 when their was a shortage of paint brushes

4. the first patent for artificial teath were granted on march 9 1822

March 10

1   the first words ever spoken over the telephone happened on this date in 1876

2. the salvation army started in the united states on march 10 1880

3. today is harriet tubman day she be born into slavery in dorchester county maryland she died on march 10 1913 shes buried in ohio

March 11

1. the first snowfall in the famous blizzard of 1888 took place on march 11 by the time it quite 40 to 50 inches of snow had fell

2. john chapman johnny appleseed a frontier hero and horticulturist died on march 11 1845

3. lorraine hansberrys a raisin in the sun became the first play by a african american women to premiere on broadway it did so on march 11 1959

March 12

1. the girl scouts of america were founded on march 12 1912
2. the united states post office department was established on this date in 1789
3. charlie bird parker a genius of modern jazz died on march 12 1955
4. american author jack kerouac was born on march 12 1922 his most famous book is called on the road
5. charles boycott born today in 1832 left his name to the english language after he issued eviction notices to his tenants they refused to have anything to do with him

March 13

1. chester greenwood patented the first earmuffs on march 13 1877

2. chicago was founded by jean baptiste pointe du sable on march 13 1773

3. won of the discoverers of oxygen was joseph priestley he was born on march 13 1733

4. the planet uranus was discovered by astronomer william herschel on this day in 1781

March 14

1. albert einstein a mathematician and physicist was born on march 14 1879 he is best known for his theory of relativity

2. eli whitney patented the cotton gin on this date in 1794

3. baseball great kirby puckett was born on march 14 1961

March 15

1. andrew jackson was born on this date in 1767 he was are seventh president and was the first to represent the plane common people instead of the rich

2. maine became the twenty three state on march 15 1820

3. the people of hinckley ohio begin to look for buzzards to arrive today these birds will beginned to build there nests

4. julius caesar was assassinated on this day in 44 b c

March 16

1. today is are forth presidents birthday james madison was born in 1751 he created the constitution and fought for the addition of the first ten amendments known as the bill of rights

2. the united states military academy was established on march 16 1802

3. comedian jerry lewis born on march 16 1926 is remembered most for his labor day telethon to raise money for muscular dystrophy

4. on march 16 1960 san antonio texas became the first major southern city to integrate lunch counters

March 17

1. singer nat king cole was born in montgomery alabama on march 17 1919

2. the camp fire girl's was founded on this date in 1910

3. today is st patricks day won of the most popular legends is that st patrick drived all the snakes out of ireland and into the see did you no that the shamrock is the national flower of ireland check you encyclopedia for more information

March 18

1. happy birthday grover cleveland you where the only president too serve two terms out of sequence you was are twenty second and twenty forth president you was born today in 1837

2 statehood was granted to hawai on march 18 1959

3. rudolph diesel born march 18 1858 was a german engineer and inventer of a engine that bares his name

4. horbert rillieux a african american scientist were born on march 18 1806 he revolutionized the sugar industry

March 19

1. today the cliff swallows make there annual journey from argentina to san juan capistrano california

2. when congress passed the standard time act on march 19 1918 it established daylight saving time

3. ptolemy an astronomer recorded the first eclipse of the moon on this day in 72 a d

March 20

1. uncle toms cabin by harriet beecher stowe was published on march 20 1852

2. fred rogers was born today in 1928 his television show mister rogers nieghborhood has been a favorite for young children since1965

3. sir isaac newton died on march 20 1727 in kensington england

March 21

1. today is the traditional date for the beginning of spring
2. benito juarez was born on march 21 1806 he is considered the george washington of mexico
3. cesar chavez was born on march 21 1927 hes none for his work for better conditions for mexican american farm workers in the southwest
4. artist randolph caldecott was born in chester england on march 21 1846 the caldecott metal is named for this artist

March 22

1. the united states granted independence to the philippines on march 22 1934

2. marcel marceau born today in 1923 is an actor who does pantomime

3. arthur schawlow and charles townes patented the first laser on march 22 1960

March 23

1. patrick henry gave his famous speech give me liberty or give me death on march 23 1775

2. roger bannister was born on march 23 1929 in 1954 he officially became the first person to run a mile in less than 4 minutes

3. elisha graves otis installed the first passenger elevator in the united states on march 23 1857

4. the first standing ovation was given on this day in 1743 king george stood to applaud a performance of handels messiah and others followed his lead

March 24

1. robert koch announced the discovery of the tuberculosis germ on march 24 1882

2. today is agriculture day

3. the first white man to explore the grand canyon from the bottom was geologist john wesley powell he was born on march 24 1834

4. one of the greatest man made disasters ever occurred on this day in 1989 when the exxon valdez oil tanker spilled over 11000000 gallons of its cargo off the coast of alaska

March 25

1. lord baltimores colonists landed in maryland on march 25 1634
2. on march 25 1965 viola liuzzo a 39 year old white civil rights worker from detroit was shot and killed by klan members on highway 80 near montgomery alabama
3. singer and songrighter aretha franklin was born today in 1942 she has recieved grammy awards for her rhythm and blues records and four her sole gospel performances
4. gutzon borglum a african sculptor was born on march 25 1871 he is best known for the mount rushmore memorial in south dakota

March 26

1. robert frost a poet was born on march 26 1874

2. sandra day o connor was born on march 26 1930 she was sworn in as a associate juge of the us supreme court on september 25 1981 she is the first women ever appointed to this high court

3. the lifeboat was patented on this day in 1845

March 27

1. german scientist wilhelm konrad roentgen discoverer of the x ray was born on march 27 1845

2. the first coast to coast color tv broadcast took place on march 27 1955

3. augusta savage died on this date in 1962 he was a great sculpture

March 28

1. gunpowder was first used in europe on march 28 1380

2. on this date in 1979 a nuclear accident took place at the three mile island power plant near harrisburg pennsylvania

3. czech educator jan amos komensky born today in 1592 wrote the first textbook in which the illustrations where as important as the text

4. on march 28 1797 the washing machine was patented by nathaniel briggs of new hampshire

March 29

1. alice parker became the first african american women to recieve a united states patent she did this on march 29 1919 after designing a heating furnace that operated on gas instead of coal

2. are ten president john tyler was born on this date in 1790

3. hyman lipman patented the first pencil with a eraser on this date in 1853

4. today is veitnam veterens day the last u s troops left vietnam on this day in 1973

March 30

1. the united states aquired alaska from russia on this date in 1867

2. the fifteen amendment providing for voting rights was ratified on march 30 1870

3. vincent van gogh was born on march 30 1853 although he was dutch he painted most of his works in the countryside of france

March 31

1. air force captain edward dwight jr became the first african american to be selected for training as a astronaut he was selected on march 31 1963

2. commodore matthew c perry arranged the open door treaty with japan on march 31 1854

3. the first national advertizement for a automobile appeared on march 31 1900 in the saturday evening post it featured the slogan authomobiles that give satisfaction

4. the eiffel tower built by alexandre gustave eiffel was completed on march 31 1889

April 1

1. beware today is april fools day this practice is thought to have originated in france before the use of the gregorian calender

2. charles r drew a research physician was born on april 1 1904

3. william harvey a english physician was born on april 1 1578 he was the first to discover the function of the heart in the circulation of blood through the body

4. the united states orbited the first weather satellite on april 1 1960

April 2

1. the us mint was established in philadelphia pennsylvania on this date in 1792 george washington provided his own household silver for the coins

2. hans christian andersen a writter for young children were born on april 2 1805

3. howard university was established on april 2 1867 its located in washington dc

April 3

1. ride em pony the pony express beginned on april 3 1860

2. washington irving a humorist and writer was born on april 3 1783

3. carter g woodson a author and historian was born today in 1875

April 4

1. our ninth president william henry harrison died on this date in 1841 only 32 days after his inauguration he was the first presidant to die while in office

2. on april 4 1818 congress decreed that the flag should have thirteen stripes and a star four each state

3. reverend martin luther king jr was assassinated in memphis tennessee on april 4 1968

4. maya angelou born on april 4 1928 wrote the book i no why the caged bird sings

April 5

1. booker taliaferro washington was born a slave on a virginia plantation on april 5 1856 he organized and served as the first president of tuskegee institute in alabama

2. joseph lister founder of modern antiseptic surgery was born on this date in 1827

3. general colin l powell was born on april 5 1937

April 6

1. due too william henry harrisons death john tylers' presidential term began on april 6 1841 tyler became the first vice presidant to be sworn in under these circumstances

2. woodrow wilson are twenty eighth presidant declared war on germany on this date in 1917 germany had sank several united states ships the us was now involved in world war 1

3. admiral robert e peary matthew henson and four eskimos reached the north pole on april 6 1909

4. the first modern olympic games was held in athens greece on april 6 1896

April 7

1. lorraine hansberry became the first african american to recieve the new york drama critics circle award she one it on april 7 1959 for her first play a raisin in the sun

2. today is world health day

3. blues singer billie holiday was born on april 7 1915 she was known as lady day

April 8

1. ponce de leon a spanish explorer landed in florida on april 8 1513

2. many people where out of work in 1935 on this day a emergency relief appropriation act was approved to provide employment to people who could carry out useful projects it was called the works progress administration

3. james tyng a catcher on the harvard baseball team wore the first face protecter on april 12 1877

April 9

1. the civil war ended on april 9 1865 when general lee surrendered to general grant

2. on april 9 1866 the first civil rights act was passed despite the veto of president andrew johnson it was designed to protect the newly freed african americans from repressive legislation it set the stage for the passage of the forteenth amendment

3. the first free public libary in the united states was established on april 9 1833

April 10

1. the us patent system was established on april 10 1790

2. today is humane day the american society for the prevention of cruelty to animals was chartered on this date in 1866

3. the first arbor day was april 10 1872 in nebraska arbor day is celebrated at different times in different states

April 11

1. spelman college was organized on april 11 1883

2. lyndon johnson signed a civil rights act on this date in 1968

3. on april 11 1947 jackie robinson became the first african american to play major league baseball he played first base for the brooklyn dodgers

April 12

1. harry s truman become presidant on april 12 1945 following the death of presidant roosevelt truman was are thirty three presidant
2. the civil war begin at fort sumter on this date in 1861
3. on april 12 1961 soviet cosmonaut yuri gagarin became the first human to orbit earth
4. on this day in 1955 dr jonas salk announced the polio vaccine he had been testing was a success

April 13

1. thomas jefferson are third presidant was born on this date in 1743

2. frank w woolworth a merchant was born on april 13 1852

3. sidney poitier was the first african american to win a oscar for best performance by an actor he won this award on april 13 1964 for his role in lilies of the field

4. the first elephant came to america on april 13 1796 it came to new york city from bengal india

April 14

1. john wilkes booth shot president lincoln on this date in 1865

2. the s s titanic sank on april 14 1912 this unsinkable boat sunk after hitting a iceburg in the north alantic it cost 1517 passengers there lives

3. pocahontas married john rolfe on april 14 1614

4. on april 14 1828 noah webster completed the american dictionary of the english language after more then twenty years of work

April 15

1. andrew johnson became are seventeen presidant on april 15 1865 following the death of presidant lincoln

2. the revolutionary war ended on april 15 1783

3. today is income tax day all state and federal income tax returns must be mailed

4. leonardo da vinci was born on april 15 1452 he painted the mona lisa and the last supper

April 16

1. wilbur wright a aviation pioneer was born on april 16 1867

2. major general benjamin o davis jr became the first african american lieutenant general in the us air force on april 16 1960

3. basketball superstar kareem abdul jabbar was born on april 16 1947

April 17

1. on april 17 1542 giovanni verrazano discovered new york harbor

2. the first ford mustang was introduced on april 17 1964

3. surveyor iii a lunar probe vehicle landed on the moon on april 17 1967 it's digging apparatus told nasa what the moons surface was like

4. on april 17 1961 the united states launched the bay of pigs invasion in cuba

42

April 18

1. paul revere ride took place on this date in 1775

2. on april 18 1906 san francisco experienced a great earthquake and fire it destroyed 10000 acres of land and killed nearly 4000 people

3. the first store equipped with public washing machines in which people could do there laundry opened on april 18 1934 in fort worth texas

April 19

1. today is patriots day the battle of lexington the first major battle of the american revolution took place on april 19 1775

2. the oklahoma city bombing a act of terrorism took place on april 19 1995 it caused 168 deaths and injured 500 people

3. the first u s automobile was built on this day in 1892

April 20

1. daniel chester french born on april 20 1850 created the statue of abraham lincoln for the lincoln memorial in washington dc

2. on april 20 1812 george clinton became the first vice president of the united states to die in office

3. on april 20 1898 pierre and marie curie uncovered the elements radium and polonium

April 21

1. the spanish american war began on april 21 1898

2. its kindergarden day friedrich froebel founder of the first kindergarden was born on this date in 1782

3. john muir a naturalist was born today in 1838

April 22

1. the first earth day was celebrated on april 22 1970 focusing attention on enviromental problems are you doing you're part in conserving and recycling

2. oklahoma opened to settlers on april 22 1889

3. the first pear of roller skates was patented on april 22 1823

April 23

1. william shakespeare was born on april 23 1564 and died on april 23 1616 he writted romeo and juliet

2. president james buchanan are fifteen president was born on this date in 1791

3. the first public showing of a motion picture took place in new york city on april 23 1896

4. on april 23 1985 coca cola introduced new coke this variation on the popular soft drink did not sell good

April 24

1. the library of congress were founded on april 24 1800

2. robert penn warren born on april 24 1905 was named poet laureate by the library of congress in 1986

3. the first american newspaper the boston news letter was published by john campbell on april 24 1704

April 25

1. guglielmo marconi inventer of wireless telegraphy was born on april 25 1874

2. a dog named buddy became the first seeing eye dog on this day in 1928

3. martin waldseemuller was a geographer and mapmaker on april 25 1507 he published a geography book on a map of the world he called a newly discovered continent america

April 26

1. john j audubon a ornithologist was born on april 26 1785

2. the nuclear accident at chernobyl ussr took place on this date in 1986

3. today is the birthday of charles richter in 1935 he developed a scale which measures the magnitude of earthquakes

---

April 27

1. ulysses simpson grant was born on this date in 1822 besides being are eighteen president he was commander of the union troops during the civil war

2. samuel morse inventer of the morse code was born on april 27 1791

3. sierra leone was proclaimed a independant nation on this date in 1961

4. ludwig bemelmans was born on april 27 1898 he is the righter of madeline

April 28

1. maryland became the seven state on april 28 1788

2. president james monroe are five president was born on this date in 1758

3. on april 28 1919 leslie ervin made the first successful parachute jump

April 29

1. on april 29 1954 baseball great willie mays was voted the most valuable player of the national league

2. swedish inventer gideon sundback patented the zipper on this date in 1913

3. william randolph hearst a newspaper publisher was born on april 29 1863

April 30

1. louisiana became the eighteen state on april 30 1812 it seceded on january 26 1861 and was re admitted in july of 1868

2. president george washington was inaugurated on this date in 1789 the inauguration took place at federal hall in new york city which was then are nations capital

3. napoleon the ruler of france concluded the largest real estate transaction in world history on april 30 1803 he sold the louisiana territory to president jefferson

4. adolf hitler died on this day in 1945

May 1

1. the empire state building was completed on this day in 1930 this new york monument is 102 stories high

2. orson welles film citizen kane premiered on may 1 1941 many film critics consider it the finest film ever made

3. on may 1 1963 james whitaker became the first american to climb mount everest.

May 2

1. the hudson bay company was chartered on may 2 1670

2. elijah mccoy born in canada on may 2 1844 invented the lubricator cup his invention dripped oil continuously to oil machinery parts so they did not have to be shut down

3. on may 2 1932 pearl s buck was awarded the pulitzer prize for fiction for her book the good earth

May 3

1. the first united states school of medicine was established in philadelphia on may 3 1765

2. the worlds columbian exposition opened in chicago on may 3 1893 often called the white city the exposition used more electricity than the hole city of chicago at that time

3. golda meir was born on may 3 1898 her family and she emigrated from kiev russia to milwaukee wisconsin she eventually became prime minister of isreal

4. the first comic book was published on this day in 1934

May 4

1. horace mann a educator was born on may 4 1796

2. today is national weather observers day

3. peter minuit landed on manhattan on may 4 1626 he eventually purchased the island from the native americans living their

4. actress audrey hepburn was born on may 4 1929

May 5

1. on may 5 1862 a group of poorly armed mexican soldiers defeated thousands of well armed professional french soldiers at puebla mexico cinco de mayo which commemorates this victory is celebrated by people of mexican decent

2. the first suborbital space flight was made by alan b shepard on may 5 1961

3. nellie bly born on may 5 1867 used the pen name elizabeth cochran she was the first america women journalist to achieve international fame

4. on this day in 1961 the federal minimum wage was raised to one dollar twenty five an hour do you know what the current federal minimum wage is

May 6

1. president dwight d eisenhower signed the civil rights act of 1960 on may 6

2. robert e peary a artic explorer was born on may 6 1856

3. the first postage stamp was issued in england on this date in 1840

4. this is the halveway point of spring their are as many days until summer begins as have passed since the last day of winter

5. hall of fame baseball player willie mays was born on may 6 1931

May 7

1. the liner lusitania was sank in the alantic ocean by a german submarine on may 7 1915

2. robert browning was born on may 7 1812 he wrote the pied piper of hamelin

3. peter ilich Tchaikovsky a famous russian composer was born on may 7 1840 sixteen years earlier on the very same day beethoven's ninth symfony debuted

4. on may 7 1959 93103 spectaters gathered at the los angeles coliseum to honor catcher roy campanella who had been paralyzed in a traffic accident a year earlier it was the largest crowd ever assembled to witness a baseball game

May 8

1. today is v e day germany surrendered on may 8 1945 ending world war ii the war began september 1 1939 when germany attacked polland

2. president harry s truman was born on may 8 1884

3. jean h dunant a swiss was born today in 1828 he founded the international red cross

4. the french celebrate joan of arc day each may 8th

May 9

1. the first comic strip was published on may 9 1754 by benjamin franklin

2. james pollard espy a meteorologist who started scientific whether prediction was born on this date in 1785

3. john brown a abolitionist was born on may 9 1800

4. james m barrie born may 9 1860 was a english author his play peter pan is set in never never land a place were know won grows up

May 10

1. its golden spike day the completion of the first transcontinental railroad happened on may 10 1869

2. their was excitement on may 10 1927 when the hotel statler in boston massachusetts offered too radio channels to guests thirteen hundred rooms where equipped with headsets but only won person could listen at a time

3. on this day in 1872 victoria woodhull became the first female to run for the office of president of the united states of america

May 11

1. minnesota became the thirty two state on may 11 1858

2. ottmar merganthaler inventer of the linotype was born on may 11 1854

3. today is the birth date of william grant still he was a composer of musicals symphonies and operas he was born in 1895

4. today in 1947 the b f goodrich company started to manufacture tubeless tires

May 12

1. florence nightingale the english founder of modern nursing was born on may 12 1820

2. may 12 1812 is the birth date of edward lear his name is synonymous with limericks

3. baseball legend yogi berra was born on may 12 1925 hes known for saying such things as it aint over til its over

May 13

1. heavy wait boxing champion joe louis was born on may 13 1914 in chambers county alabama

2. the united states declared war on mexico on may 13 1846

3. jamestown virginia the first permanent english settlement in north america was founded on may 13 1607

4. singer stevie wonder was born on may 13 1951

May 14

1. gabriel d fahrenheit was born on may 14 1686 his system marks 32 degrees as the freezing point and 212 degrees as boiling

2. lois and clark began exploring louisiana and the northwest territories on this day in 1804

3. its midnight sun at north cape from may 14 until july 30 the son never goes below the horizon at this island

4. on may 14 1908 charles w furnas became the first passenger to fly in a airplain he flew with wilbur wright

May 15

1. the first airmale service flight took place on may 15 1918
2. gertrude elise ayer was the first female african american public school principle in new york she became principle on may 15 1935
3. ellen church a trained nurse became the first airplain stewardess on this date in 1930
4. on this date in 1940 the first successful helicopter flight in the u s took place
5. l frank baum author of the wonderful wizard of oz 1900 was born on may 15 1856

May 16

1. elizabeth peabody was born on may 16 1804 she is the founder of the first united states kindergarden

2. on may 16 1866 congress authorized the creation of the nickle

3. the first academy awards ceremony was held on this date in 1929

May 17

1. father jacques marquette and louis joliet began exploring the mississippi river on may 17 1673

2. happy birthday new york stock exchange on may 17 1792 about too dozen merchants and brokers agreed to form a group four buying and selling stocks

3. the landmark supreme court decision in the case brown vs board of education of topeka kansas was declared on may 17 1954 this ruling stated that racial segregation in public schools was unconstitutional

May 18

1. mount st helens erupted on may 18 1980 causing loss of life fires mud slides and floods

2. the canadian city of montreal was founded on this day in 1642

3. on may 18 1852 massachusetts became the first state to pass a law which made school attendance mandatory for school age children

May 19

1. the ringling brothers circus opened in baraboo wisconsin on may 19 1884

2. malcolm x was born malcolm little on may 19 1925 he becomed famous as a leader of the black religious movement named the nation of islam

3. mary mcleod bethune a dedicated educator and civic leader died on may 19 1955 in daytona beach florida

4. today is dark day in new england at midday in 1780 the sky in new england suddenly becomed dark know won is sure why this happened

May 20

1. the homestead act was signed on may 20 1862

2. dolley payne madison wife of the forth president was born on may 20 1768 she famous for saving the portrait of george washington when the british burned the capital in 1812

3. amelia earhart began the first solo flight by a women on may 20 1932

May 21

1. the american red cross was organized on may 21 1881 clara barton a civil war nurse was it's founder

2. the first bicycles where imported into the united states on may 21 1891

3. charles a lindbergh completed his first solo transalantic flight on this date in 1927

4. glenn h curtiss born on may 21 1878 helped design the first plane sold commercially it was called the june bug in 1909 it sold for $5000

May 22

1. the savannah the first american ship made the transatlantic crossing under steam power it started from savannah georgia on may 22 1819 the trip to liverpool england took 29 days

2. benjamin o davis jr of the united states air force became the first african american in u s military history to be promoted to the rank of major general this happened on may 22 1959

3. sir arthur conan doyle was born on may 22 1859 he created the famous detective sherlock holmes

May 23

1. south carolina was the eight state to ratify the constitution it did so on may 23 1788 it than seceded on december 20 1860 and was re admitted in 1868

2. carolus linnaeus was born on this day in 1707 he is known as the father of biology

3. on may 23 1975 junko tabei a japanese house wife become the first women to reach the top of mt everest

May 24

1. samuel f b morse sent the first telegraph message on may 24 1844

2. today marks the death of edward kennedy duke ellington he died on this date in 1974

3. on may 24 1983 hundreds of people walked across the brooklyn brige in new york city they where celebrating the 100 anniversery of the opening of this brige to traffic

May 25

1. ralph waldo emerson a philosopher and writter was born on may 25 1803

2. The film star wars premiered on may 25 1977

3. on may 25 1986 7000000 people participated in hands across america the purpose of the demonstration was to bring attention to the problem of homelessness in america

May 26

1. paine college was founded in augusta georgia on may 26 1864

2. the last confederate troops in the civil war surrendered in shreveport louisiana on may 26 1865

3. actor john wayne was born today in 1907

4. sally kirsten ride was born in encino california on may 26 1951 on january 16 1978 she became the first women candidate to become a astronaut

May 27

1. the golden gate brige opened in san francisco on may 27 1937

2. julia ward howe author of the battle hymn of the republic was born on this date in 1819

3. isadora duncan a dancer was born on may 27 1878

May 28

1. booker t washington became the first african american to be elected to the hall of fame of great americans it happened on may 28 1945

2. john muir formed the sierra club on may 28 1892

3. jim thorpe born on may 28 1886 was won of the worlds most versatile athletes he played professional football one fame as a track and field champion and played major league baseball

May 29

1. president john fitzgerald kennedy was born may 29 1917 in brookline massachusets a suberb of boston jack as his family called him was are thirty five president

2. rhode island became the thirteen state of the union on may 29 1790

3. wisconsin became the thirty state on may 29 1848

4. patrick henry a american revolution leader and orator was born on may 29 1736

May 30

1. know one no's exactly when memorial day was first observed according to tradition memorial day originated during the civil war when some sothern woman choose may 30 to decorate soldiers graves

2. christopher columbus began his third voyage on may 30 1498

3. the lincoln memorial was dedicated on may 30 1922 its located in washington dc

4. the compact disc was first introduced in 1981

May 31

1. on may 31 1819 walt whitman a american poet was born old he wrote leaves of grass

2. today is indianapolis 500 race day

3. the united states copyright law was enacted on may 31 1790

4. on may 31 1933 a patent was given to gerald brown for making invisible glass the patent was for a process that would reduce the amount of reflection on glass windows

June 1

1. kentucky achieved statehood on june 1 1792 it was the second to do so after the original thirteen colonies

2. tennessee became the sixteen state on june 1 1796 it seceded on june 24 1861 and was re admitted on july 24 1866

3. jacues marquette an french explorer was born on june 1 1637

4. brigham young leader of the mormons was born on this date in 1801

June 2

1. on june 2 1875 alexander graham bell herd a sound on his invention the telephone

2. a swimming pool built in the white house was formally accepted and opened by president franklin roosevelt on june 2 1933

3. on this day in 1941 baseball great lou gehrig died at age 37 of a disease which now bears his name at his retirement ceremony gehrig said today i consider myself the luckiest man on the face of the earth

June 3

1. jefferson davis president of the confederate states of america was born on june 3 1808

2. dr charles drew was born on this date in 1904 he was a blood plasma researcher

3. the ballad casey at the bat was first printed in the san francisco examiner on june 3 1888

4. the new york knickerbockers a baseball team introduced the first baseball uniforms on june 3 1851

June 4

1. on june 4 1896 henry ford introduced his first car the quadra cycle

2. the first baptist church in america was founded on june 4 1665

3. on june 4 1781 jack jouett rode 45 miles and 6 1/2 ours to warn virginia governor thomas jefferson and the legislature that the british where comming

4. on june 4 1965 major ed white became the first american to walk in space

June 5

1. senator robert f kennedy was shot by a assassin on june 5 1968

2. on june 5 1956 the federal courts ruled that segregation on the montgomery city buses were unconstitutional

3. the first hot air balloon flight by the montgolfier brothers took place in france on june 5 1783

4. today is world enviroment day activities are held to show concern for the preservation and enhancement of the enviroment

June 6

1. today is d day on june 6 1944 the british canadians and americans invaded the beaches of normandy

2. on june 6 1932 the us government passed a law that placed a tax of won scent a gallon on gasoline and other motor fuel

3. on this day in 1872 susan b anthony was fined for trying to vote at that time women were not allowed to vote

June 7

1. gwendolyn brooks was born on june 7 1917 she is a well none black poet

2. a horse named gallant fox won the belmont stakes on this day in 1930 with this victory gallant fox became only the second horse to win the triple crown of horse racing

3. to capture the triple crown in horse racing a horse has to win the preakness stakes the kentucky derby and the belmont stakes in the same year

June 8

1. frank lloyd wright a architect was born on june 8 1869

2. on june 8 1953 the supreme court banned discrimination in restaurants in washington dc

3. barbara bush wife of presidant george bush was born today in 1925

4. ice cream was first advertized and sold in america on june 8 1786

June 9

1. meta vaux warwick fuller the foremost african american sculptress in the 19 century was born on june 9 1877

2. cole porter a composer was born on june 9 1893

3. donald duck appeared in a short cartoon on june 9 1934

June 10

1. jack johnson the first african american heavy wait boxing champion died on june 10 1946

2. maurice sendak was born today in 1928 he is the illustrator and author of many books including were the wild things are

3. the first drive through restaurant opened on this day in 1952

June 11

1. french oceanographer jacques cousteau was born on june 11 1910

2. jeannette rankin was born near missoula montana on june 11 1880 she was the first women to be elected to the us house of representatives

3. quarterback joe montana was born on june 11 1956 he lead the san francisco 49ers to four super bowl victories

June 12

1. medgar evers was assassinated on june 12 1963 at the time he was head of the mississippi naacp

2. today is the celebration of the invention of baseball it was named for the for bases the batter must touch to score a run

3. george bush are fourty one president was born on june 12 1924

4. on june 12 1967 a soviet space capsule landed on the surface of planet venus

June 13

1. the department of labor was created on june 13 1888

2. football hero red grange was born on june 13 1903 he was nicknamed the galloping ghost

3. on june 13 1966 the us supreme court ruled that when someone is arrested he or she dont have to say nothing until a lawyer is present these our called the miranda rights

June 14

1. today is flag day flags have been used since ancient times as symbols

2. harriet beecher stowe author of uncle toms cabin was born on june 14 1811

3. congress established the united states army on june 14 1775

June 15

1. arkansas becomed the twenty five state on june 15 1836 it seceded on may 6 1861 and was re admitted on june 22 1868

2. ben franklins historic kite flying experiment proving lighting was composed of electricity took place on june 15 1752

3. the magna carta was granted by king john on june 15 1215

4. the first non stop tranalantic flight arrived in ireland on june 15 1919

5. henry o flipper became the first African american graduate of west point on june 15 1877

June 16

1. the ford motor company was founded on june 16 1903

2 james joyces famous novel ulysses tells the story of one day in the life of three different people that day is june 16 1904

3. the first women in space valentina tereshkova spoke these words on june 16 1963 it is i sea gull she was a twenty six year old soviet cosmonaut at the time

June 17

1. the battle of bunker hill began on june 17 1775

2. explorers father jacques marquette & louis joliet discovered the mississippi river on june 17 1673

3. on june 17 1972 five burglars was arrested for being in the offices of the democratic national committee in the watergate building in washington dc

4. barry manilow was born on june 17 1946 he be none as an singer composer and arranger

June 18

1. napoleon was defeated at waterloo on june 18 1815

2. on june 18 1988 forteen students at hanover high school new hampshire made the guiness book of world records by playing leapfrog they played for ate days thats 189 hours and 49 minutes at a distance of 888.1 miles

3. sally kirsten ride became the first american women in space on june 18 1983

4. comic strip character garfield appeared for the first time on june 18 1978

June 19

1. on june 19 1885 the statue of liberty arrived in the new york harbor from france

2. the first recorded baseball game was played at elysian fields in hoboken new jersey on june 19 1846

3. fathers day was first celebrated in spokane washington on june 19 1910

June

June 20

1. west virginia become the thirty five state on june 20 1863

2. congress adopted the design for the great seal of the us on june 20 1782

3. eli whitney applied for the patent of the cotton gin on june 20 1793

4. to celebrate the comming summer season fairbanks alaska has a midnight sun baseball game that begins about 10:30 pm and is played without artificial lights

June 21

1. new hampshire was the nine state to ratify the united states constitution it did so on june 21 1787

2. daneil carter beard was born on june 21 1850 he was an naturalist righter illustrater and founder of the boy scouts in the us

3. today are the traditional date for the beginning of summer

June 22

1. the department of justice was founded on june 22 1870

2. on june 22 1970 the us adopted the twenty six amendment which lowered the voting age from 21 to 18

3. on june 22 1943 web dubois became the first african american to be elected to membership in the national institute of arts and letters

4. journalist ed bradley from 60 minutes was born today in 1941

June 23

1. william penn signed a treaty with the indians on june 23 1683

2. irving s cobb born june 23 1876 was a humorous righter of short stories and novels he believed that you had to poke fun at yourself before you could poke fun at anyone else without hurting his feelings

3. olympic track star wilma rudolph was born on june 23 1940

June 24

1. john cabot discovered north americas mainland on june 24 1497

2. henry ward beecher a clergyman and orator was born on this date in 1813

3. gustavus franklin swift was born on this date in 1839 he was 17 when he went into the butchering business in 1875 swift went to chicago and opened the first slaughterhouse

4. john ciardi one of americas foremost contemporary poets was born on june 24 1916

June 25

1. general george custers forces was destroyed by sioux and cheyenne indians at little big horn on june 25 1876 in montana the indians was lead by sitting bull

2. virginia was the ten state to ratify the constitution it did so on june 25 1788 it seceded on april 17 1861 and was re admitted on january 26 1870

3. the korean war began on june 25 1950

4. on june 25 1941 president roosevelt created the committee on fair employment practices

June 26

1. the united nations charter was signed on june 26 1945

2. novelist pearl s buck was born on this date in 1892

3. on june 26 1959 the st lawrence seaway was dedicated and officially opened

4. babe didrikson zaharias one of the greatest female atheletes of all time was born on june 26 1911 babe excelled at several sports

June 27

1. today is the birth date of helen keller she was born on this date in 1880

2. poet paul laurence dunbar was born on june 27 1872

3. james smithson who died today in 1829 left his great wealth to start a museum in washington dc that museum is called the smithsonian institution

June 28

1. archduke francis ferdinand of austria was assassinated on june 28 1914 this was the start of world war 1

2. the versailles treaty was signed on june 28 1918 world war 1 was officially over

3. john elway longtime quarterback of the denver broncos was born on june 28 1960 elway holds the record for most victories by a quarterback in professional football history

June 29

1. george w goethals the engineer who supervised the building of the panama canal was born on june 29 1858

2. william james mayo was born on this date in 1861 he was the surgeon who helped establish the mayo foundation

3. as a college freshman charles dumas becomed the first person to make a high jump of seven foot one halve inch he did it on this date in 1956

4. born in seigen germany on june 29 1577 peter paul rubens become won of the greatest flemish painters of the 1600

June 30

1. zaire was proclaimed a independant nation on june 30 1960

2. the pure food and drug act was signed on this date in 1906

3. on june 30 1940 the us fish and wildlife service was established

4. on june 30 1908 a huge meteorite landed in central siberia people as far away as 466 miles saw it in fool daylight the blast was felt 50 miles away

5. bondin crossed niagra falls on a rope 1100 foot long on june 30 1859

July 1

1. somali was proclaimed a independant nation on july 1 1960

2. the first us postage stamps was issued on this date in 1847

3. the battle of gettysburg began on july 1 1863

4. today is dominion day the dominion of canada were established on july 1 1863

July 2

1. lyndon baines johnson are thirty six presidant signed the civil rights bill on july 2 1964 martin luther king jr was present for this momentous occasion

2. supreme court justice thurgood marshall was born on july 2 1908

3. the continental congress declared us independence from england on july 2 1776

4. president james garfield was assassinated on this date in 1881

July 3

1. idaho become the fourty three state on july 3 1890

2. john singleton copley a painter was born on july 3 1738

3. george m cohan a composer was born on this date in 1878

July 4

1. thomas jefferson died on this date in 1826 coincidentally its the anniversery of the declaration of independance which was written in 1776

2. calvin coolidge are thirtyith presidant was born on july 4 1872 he was vice president to president harding and took office following hardings death on august 2 1923

3. stephen foster a composer was born on july 4 1826

July 5

1. david g farragut was born on july 5 1801 he was the first admiral of the us navy

2. phineas taylor barnum was born on july 5 1810 he be a showman and circus promoter

3. on july 5 1975 arthur ashe became the first african american to win the mens tennis singles championship at wimbledon

July 6

1. malawi was proclaimed a independant nation on july 6 1964

2. naval hero john paul jones was born on july 6 1747

3. the republican party was named on july 6 1854

4. beatrix potter creator of peter rabbit was born on this date in 1866

5. the first all star baseball game took place on july 6 1933 legend has it that on that day babe ruth pointed to the outfield fence before hitting a home run there on the very next pitch

July 7

1. hawai was annexed by the united states on july 7 1898

2. carlo lorenzini whose pen name was carlo collodi published the first chapter of his classic tail pinocchio on july 7 1881

3. sandra day o conner was the first women justice of the united states supreme court she was sworn in on july 7 1981

July 8

1. while tolling the death of chief justice john marshall on july 8 1835 the liberty belle cracked

2. the wall street journal was first published on july 8 1889

3. the first ice cream sunday was served on this day in 1881

July 9

1. are twelfth presidant zachary taylor died on this date in 1850 he had only been in office for sixteen months when he suffered a sonstroke while takeing part in the ceremonies at the then unfinished washington monument on the forth of july

2. john d rockefeller sr a industrialist and philanthropist was born on july 9 1839

3. elias howe was born on this date in 1819 he patented the sewing machine in 1846

July 10

1. millard fillmore took the presidensy after the death of zachary taylor he be are thirteen president he modernized the white house bye putting in the first bath tub with running water and adding a room for a libary

2. wyoming become the forty four state on july 10 1890

3. on july 10 1790 washington dc were chosen as the sight of our nations capitle

4. mary bethune a educater was born on july 10 1875

July 11

1. president john quincy adams was born on july 11 1767

2. the us air force academy was established on july 11 1955

3. elwyn brooks white was born on july 11 1899 he is best known as e b white author of stuart little 1945 charlottes web 1952 and the trumpet of the swan 1970

July 12

1. george eastman a photography pioneer was born on july 12 1854

2. the metal of honor was established on july 12 1861

3. aaron burr killed alexander hamilton in a duel on july 12 1804

4. comedian bill cosby was born on july 12 1938 and american writer henry david thoreau was born on july 12 1817

July 13

1. congress passed the northwest ordinance on july 13 1787

2. woman beginned competing in the olympics on july 13 1908

3. erno rubik inventer of the rubiks cube was born on july 13 1944

July 14

1. gerald rudolph ford are thirty eight president was born on july 14 1913 he was the first vice president not elected by the people to become president this followed the resignation of president nixon

2. today is bastille day independance day in france on july 14 1789 the people of paris captured the bastille an old fortress and prison

3. edwin james make his ascent of pikes peak on july 14 1820

July 15

1. wiley post began his first round the world solo flight on july 15 1933

2. clement moore author of a visit from st nicholas was born on this date in 1779

3. on this day in 1965 congress passed a law which required all cigarette packages to display a health warning

July 16

1. alamogordo new mexico was the dessert area used as a experimental drop sight for the first atomic bomb the bomb was dropped on july 16 1945 the mushroom cloud rose 41000 feet into the air it left a halve mile wide crater with a glassy radioactive crust

2. roald amundsen a norwegian explorer and discoverer of the south pole was born on july 16 1872

3. arnold adoff was born on july 16 1935 in november of 1988 adoff recieved the eighth national council of teachers of english award for excellence in poetry for children

July 17

1. john jacob astor financier and fur merchant was born on july 17 1763

2. spain ceded florida to the united states on july 17 1819

3. disneyland was founded on this day in 1955

July 18

1. tennis was introduced in the united states on july 18 1874

2. the presidential succession act was signed on july 18 1947

3. at the age of 14 nadia comaneci became the first gymnast to recieve a perfect score in the olympic games it happened on july 18 1976

July 19

1. the first woman rights convention was held in seneca falls new york on july 19 1848

2. samuel colt inventer of the repeating pistol was born on this date in 1814

3. poet eve merriam was born on july 19 1916

4. karla kuskin a native new yorker and a righter of prose and poetry was born on july 19 1932

July

July 20

1. on july 20 1969 united states astronaut neil a armstrong commander of the apollo 11 become the first person to set foot on the moon he said that's one small step for man one giant leap for mankind

2. the first draft number of world war 1 was drawn on july 20 1917

3. georgia joined the colonies on july 20 1770

July 21

1. the first battle of bull run took place on july 21 1861

2. the us veterans administration was established on july 21 1930

3. actor and comedian robin williams was born today in 1952

July 22

1. moses cleveland founded cleveland ohio on july 22 1796

2. alexander mackenzie was the first man to cross north america he reached the pacific ocean on july 22 1793

3. poet carl sandburg died on july 22 1967

4. emma lazarus writed the poem for the statue of liberty she be born on july 22 1849

July 23

1. the first typewriter was patented on july 23 1829

2. the bunker hill monument was completed on this date in 1841

3. general william booth founded the salvation army in england on july 23 1865

4. the ice cream cone was introduced at st louis worlds fair on july 23 1904

July 24

1. amelia earhart was born on july 24 1897 she was a aviator writer and lecturer

2. salt lake city utah was founded on july 24 1847 by a group of mormons led by brigham young

3. on july 24 1783 simon bolivar was born he is known as the father of these five countries venezuela ecuador columbia peru and bolivia

July 25

1. the continent of antartica was discovered on july 25 1820

2. puerto rico becomed a commonwealth on july 25 1952

3. on this day in 1983 the temperature in antartica dipped to 129 degrees below zero that is the lowest natural temperature ever recorded

July 26

1. new york becomed the eleven state to ratify the constitution it did so on july 26 1788

2. the us postal service began on july 26 1775

3. on july 26 1965 great britain granted independence to the maldive islands which lie for hundred miles southwest of ceylon in the indian ocean

July 27

1. the first successful transalantic cable was completed on july 27 1866

2. the us state department was established on this date in 1789

3. the korean armistice was signed on july 27 1953

July 28

1. world war 1 beginned on july 28 1914

2. the 14 amendment to the constitution was effective on july 28 1868

3. today is national joseph lee day we are honoring the founder of playgrounds

4. skylab 2 was launched from cape kennedy florida on july 28 1973 the crew spent a record breaking 59 days in space cape kennedy is now called cape canaveral

July 29

1. booth tarkington a novelist was born on july 29 1869

2. president eisenhower signed the national aeronautics and space act nasa on this day in 1958

3. the international atomic energy agency was established on july 29 1957

July 30

1. the first representative assembly in america took place in jamestown virginia on july 30 1619

2. henry ford auto manufacturer and philanthropist was born on july 30 1863

3. in god we trust became a official us motto on july 30 1956

4. actor arnold schwarzenegger was born on july 30 1947 in austria

July 31

1. the first us patent was granted on july 31 1790 it was granted to samuel hopkins of vermont for a soap making process using potash and pearl ash

2. american president george bush and soviet president mikhail gorbachev signed the strategic arms reduction treaty on this day in 1991

3. construction began on the u s mint in washington d c on this day in 1792

August 1

1. herman melville author of moby dick was born on august 1 1819

2. colorado became the thirty eight state on august 1 1876

3. the u s army air force was extablished on august 1 1907

4. francis scott key author of the star spangled banner was born today in 1779

August 2

1. inventer andrew hallidie piloted san franciscos first cable car down nob hill at 5:00 am on august 2 1873

2. the us bought the first military plane from the wright brothers' on august 2 1909

3. james baldwin a novelist and essayist was born in harlem new york on august 2 1924 ·

August 3

1. the country of niger was proclaimed a independant nation on august 3 1960

2. columbus sailed westward from spain on august 3 1492 the voyage was made aboard the niña pinta and santa maria

3. the uss nautilus became the first ship to reach the north pole it did so on august 3 1958

August 4

1. the us coast guard was established on august 4 1790

2. president jimmy carter signed the energy organization act on this day in 1977

3. federal income tax was first collected in the united states on august 4 1862

August 5

1. upper volta was proclaimed a independant nation on august 5 1960

2. actress marilyn monroe died on this day in 1962

3. neil armstrong was born on august 5 1930 what accomplishment was he the first person to acheive

August 6

1. the atomic bomb was dropped on hiroshima japan on august 6 1945

2. on august 6 1926 gertrude ederle became the first women to swim the english channel

3. president lyndon b johnson signed the voting rights act on this day in 1965

August 7

1. the international peace bridge was dedicated on august 7 1927 this commemorated the long lasting peace between the us and canada

2. george stephenson invented the steam locomotive on august 7 1815

3. ralph bunche statesmen social scientist diplomat united nations representative and winner of the nobel peace prize was born on august 7 1904 in detroit michigan

August 8

1. the ivory coast was proclaimed a independant nation on august 8 1960

2. marjorie kinnan rawlings a novelist was born on august 8 1896

3. today is intertribal indian ceremonial day the ceremony takes place in gallup new mexico

4. a artificial heart pump was successfully implanted for the first time on august 8 1966

August 9

1. our thirty seven president richard milhous nixon was the first president ever to resign from office he resigned on august 9 1974 do to the watergate scandle

2. english righter izaak walton none as the father of angling was born on august 9 1593

3. on august 9 1945 the us dropped a atomic bomb on nagasaki japan

4. baseball football player deion sanders was born on august 9 1967

August 10

1. missouri became the twenty for state on august 10 1821

2. president herbert c hoover are thirty one president was born on august 10 1874

3. the smithsonian institution was established in washington dc on august 10 1846

August 11

1. chad was proclaimed a independant nation on august 11 1960

2. the nation of chad is located on the continent of africa

3. alex haley author of the pulitzer prize winning novel roots was born on august 11 1921

August 12

1. the first police force was established in american on august 12 1658

2. thomas edison invented the phonograph on this date in 1877

3. isaac singer patented his sewing machine on this date in 1851

August 13

1. manilla surrendered to us forces on august 13 1898

2. lucy stone a womans rights leader was born on august 13 1818

3. sharpshooter annie oakley was born on this date in 1860

August 14

1. the social security act was approved on august 14 1935

2. julia child a famous chef was born on aughust 14 1912

3. the atlantic charter was issued on this date in 1941 by american president franklin d roosevelt and british prime minister winston churchill

August 15

1. japan surrendered on august 15 1945 after the atomic bomb was dropped on the city of hiroshima and than nagasaki world war ii had ended

2. congo brazzaville was proclaimed a independant nation on august 15 1960

3. the panama canal was opened on this date in 1914

4. napoleon bonaparte was born on august 15 1769

5. the famous woodstock music festival began on this day in 1969 it lasted three days

August 16

1. the battle of bennington virginia took place on august 16 1777

2. elvis presley died on this day in 1977 his home in memphis tennessee is called graceland

3. pop singer madonna was born on august 16 1958

August 17

1. gabon was proclaimed a independant nation on august 17 1960

2. davy crockett frontiersmen scout and politician was born on august 17 1786

3. robert fultons steamboat the clermont made a successful run up the hudson river in new york on august 17 1807

4. gold was discovered in the klondike on this date in 1896

August 18

1. on august 18 1587 virginia dare became the first child born in america to english parents

2. meriwether lewis a explorer was born on this date in 1774

3. baseball player roberto clemente was born on august 18 1934

August 19

1. today is national aviation day orville wright inventer and airplane manufacturer was born on august 19 1871

2. ogden nash a writer of lite verse was born on august 19 1902

3. bill clinton the 42nd president of the united states of america was born on this day in 1946

August 20

1. benjamin harrison are twenty third president was born into politics on this date in 1833 his father was a congressman from ohio his grandfather was are ninth president and his great grandfather signed the declaration of independance

2. senegal was proclaimed a independant nation on august 20 1960

3. naval hero oliver h perry was born on this date in 1785

4. in music history tchaikovskys 1812 overture premiered on this day in 1882

August 21

1. hawaii was proclaimed are fifty state on august 21 1959 it is made up of 132 islands including the ate main islands

2. the lincoln douglas debates began on august 21 1858

3. on august 21 1967 the u s defense department announced that two of its jets bound for north vietnam had been shot down over the peoples republic of china

August 22

1. the first local chapter of the american red cross was founded on august 22 1881 by clara barton

2. on august 22 1989 nolan ryan became the first pitcher in major leauge baseball history to strike out 5000 batters in a career

3. on this day in 1902 theodore roosevelt became the first prezident to ride in a automobile

August 23

1. edgar lee masters poet and biographer was born on august 23 1869

2. on this day in 1927 nicola sacco and bartolomeo vanzetti were executed in massachusettes for a crime that some felt the two did not commit

3. on august 23 1989 victoria brucker of san pedro california became the first girl to play in a little league world series game

August 24

1. the white house was burned by the british on august 24 1814

2. a volcanoe in italy mt vesuvius buried pompeii under a thick blanket of ash after erupting on august 24 ad 79

3. the waffle iron was patented on this day in 1869

4. baseball player cal ripken jr who holds the record for most consecutive games played was born on august 24 1960

August 25

1. leonard bernstein composer and conductor was born on this date in 1918

2. bret harte author and poet was born on august 25 1836

3. scottish actor sean connery was born on august 25 1930 he is best known for playing james bond in several movies

August 26

1. today is womans equality day the nineteenth amendment granting woman the write to vote was adopted on august 26 1920

2. on august 26 1903 the first automobile arrived in new york city after 52 days of travell across the us

3. the first televised baseball game took place on this day in 1939 the teams that faced each other on that day were the cincinnati reds and the brooklyn dodgers

August 27

1. the first radio message was sent from a airplane on august 27 1910

2. president lyndon b johnson are thirty six president was born on august 27 1908

3. the first oil well was drilled in the united states on august 27 1859 at titusville pennsylvania

August 28

1. the first cole was mined in the us on august 28 1922

2. the first united states commercial radio broadcast took place on august 28 1922

3. more than 200000 americans marched in washington dc on august 28 1963 for civil rights among the leaders of the march was jesse jackson and the reverend dr martin luther king jr

August 29

1. on august 29 1957 congress passed the first civil rights act since 1875

2. oliver wendell holmes was born on august 29 1809 he write poettry and essayies

3. pop star michael jackson was born on august 29 1958 in gary indiana

August 30

1. mary wollstonecraft shelley author of frankenstein was born on august 30 1797

2. guion bluford jr became the first african american astronot in space on this day in 1983

3. an emergency communications link between washington d c and moscow first went into operation on august 30 1963

August 31

1. thomas edison patented the kinetoscope on this day in 1887

2. the agricultural hall of fame was established on august 31 1960

3. the u s department of housing and urban development was established on august 31 1965

September 1

1. world war 2 beginned on september 1 1939 when germany attacked polland

2. on september 1 1985 dr robert ballard discovered the titanic sitting upright on the ocean bottom 2.5 miles below the surface

3. in 1998 a movie based on the sinking of the titanic won an academy award for best picture the movie called titanic cost over 100 million dollars to make

September 2

1. world war 2 ended on september 2 1945 less than a month after the allies dropped atomic bombs on hiroshima and nagasaki japan

2. the united states department of the treasury were established on september 2 1789

3. today in 1965 the musical group the beatles released the song yesterday

September 3

1. the signing of the treaty of paris officially ended the revolutionary war on september 3 1783

2. among other things the treaty of paris estabilished the united states geographical borders

3. viking 2 landed on mars to collect scientific data on this date in 1976

September 4

1. transcontinental television service beginned with the telecast of the japanese peace conference it took place on september 4 1951

2. george eastman recieved a patent for the first roll camera on this date in 1880

3. its newspaper carrier day in 1833 barney flaherty became the first news boy in the united states

4. baseball player mike piazza was born on september 4 1968

September 5

1. the first continental congress met at carpenters hall on september 5 1774

2. jesse james a desperado was born on this date in 1847

3. the first monday in september is labor day its observed to honor american workers the first labor day parade was held on september 5 1882

September 6

1. president william mckinley was assassinated on september 6 1901

2. jane addams a pioneer social worker and nobel peace prize winner was born today in 1860 she founded hull house in chicago in 1889 it was one of the first settlement houses in the united states

3. marquis de lafayette a french patriot was born on this date in 1757

September 7

1. thomas gregora a eleven year old english boy crawled ashore at shakespeare beach on september 7 1860 he set a record as the youngest person to swim the english channel

2. brazil became a independant nation on september 7 1822

3. queen elizabeth 1 of england was born on september 7 1533

4. anna mary robertson moses was born on september 7 1860 shes none as grandma moses and she started to paint in 1938 at age 78

September 8

1. today is international literacy day to celebrate reed a book

2. the plege of allegance was published on september 8 1892

3. st augustine florida was founded on this date in 1565 its the oldest city in the united states

4 on 9 8 98 mark mcgwire of the st louis cardinals hit his 62nd home run of the season breaking the previous mark of 61 set in 1961 mcgwire finished the year with an amazing 70 home runs

September 9

1. california becommed the thirty first state on september 9 1850

2. edward e kleinschmidt born on september 9 1875 invented the teletype printer his printer transmitted words through telephone wires

3. poet aileen fisher was born on september 9 1906

4. president ford granted a unconditional pardon to former president nixon on september 9 1974

September 10

1. oliver h perry a united states naval officer one the battle of lake erie on september 10 1813

2. elias howe patented the sewing machine on september 10 1846

3. guernica a famous painting by pablo picasso arrived in spain for the first time on september 10 1981 picasso a spanish artist did not want this piece to be seen in spain until the country was no longer ruled by francisco franco

September 11

1. alexander hamilton was appointed the first secretary of the department of the treasury on this day in 1789

2. henry hudson sailed up the hudson river on september 11 1609

3. william sydney porter was born on september 11 1862 using the pen name o henry he wrote many short storys

September 12

1. hurricane frederic struck the gulf coast on september 12 1979 its winds which reached 130 mph caused over 1 point 5 billion dollars in damage

2. richard hoe inventer of the rotary press was born on september 12 1812

3. the soviet union launched the first rocket to the moon on this date in 1959

September 13

1. milton s hershey the candy bar maker was born on this date in 1857
2. commodore john barry father of the united states navy died on this date in 1803
3. walter reed was born on september 13 1851 this physician proved that a mosquito transmitted a deadly disease called yellow fever
4. james cleveland jesse owens was born on september 13 1913 he is won of the most famous athletes in sports history he one for gold medals in the 1936 olympics in berlin germany

September 14

1. Theodore Roosevelt are twenty sixth presidant took office on september 14 1901 following the assassination of president mckinley

2. francis scott key wrote the star spangled banner on september 14 1814 he become inspired while watching the british bombardment of fort mchenry in the chesapeake bay

3. the american philatelic society was formed on this date in 1886 philatelists is people who collect stamps

4. hurricane gilbert roared into the gulf of mexico on september 14 1988 at times its winds exceeded 200 miles a our

September 15

1. william howard taft was born on september 15 1857 in cincinnati ohio he became our twenty seven president and was latter appointed chief justice of the united states supreme court

2. james fenimore cooper auther of tails of frontier life was born today in 1789

3. agatha christie is remembered as a author of famous mysteries she was born on september 15 1890

September 16

1. mexicos independence day took place on september 16 1810

2. james j hill a financier and railroad builder was born on this date in 1838

3. the mayflour departed on september 16 1620 from plymouth england their where 102 passengers aboard heading for the new world

September 17

1. baron von steuben a german military officer who fought in the american revolution was born today in 1730

2. the united states constitution was signed on september 17 1787 in philadelphia pennsylvania it went into affect nine months later on june 21 1788 it was signed by 39 delegates and replaced the articles of confederation

3. the first ten amendment to the u s constitution are called the bill of rights

September 18

1. the united states air force became a seperate military service on this date in 1947

2. president washington laid the cornerstone of the capital building on september 18 1793

3. the fugitive slave bill was passed on september 18 1850 it required that escaped slaves be returned to there owners

4. samuel johnson a english author and dictionary maker was born on september 18 1709

September 19

1. are twenty president james abram garfield died on this date in 1881 he was shot by charles guiteau garfield was president for fewer then four months

2. president washingtons farewell address was published on september 19 1796

3. a cartone staring mickey mouse was shown four the first time on september 19 1928

September 20

1. ferdinand magellan left spain on september 20 1519 to find a new route to the spice islands won of his ships was the first to circle the globe

2. alexander the great was born on september 20 356 bc

3. in a highly publicized tennis match female tennis player billie jean king won mail tennis player bobby riggs in three sets on this date in 1973

September 21

1. louis joliet a french fur trader and explorer was born on september 21 1645

2. today marks the beginning of autumn

3. on september 21 1988 dr lauro f cavazos becomed the first person of hispanic decent to serve as a cabinet member

September 22

1. michael faraday a english scientist and pioneer in electricity was born on september 22 1791

2. the british put nathan hale to death as a spy on this date in 1776 he is remembered for saying i only regret that I have but one life to lose for my country

3. italo marchiony applied for a patent for the ice cream cone on september 22 1903 it was issued on december 15 1903

September 23

1. euripides the last of the three most famous greek dramatists of the ancient world was born on september 23 480 bc

2. augustus caesar the first roman emperor was born on september 23 63 bc

3. captain john paul jones captured the serapis a british warship on this date in 1779

4. william mcguffey compiler of mcguffeys eclectic readers was born on september 23 1800

5. the planet neptune was discovered on september 23 1846

September 24

1. on september 24 1906 devils tower wyoming become the first national monument in the united states

2. the united states supreme court was created on september 24 1789

3. john marshall a united states supreme court chief justice was born on this date in 1755

4. jim henson creater of the muppets was born on september 24 1936

September 25

1. european vasco nunez de balboa cited the pacific ocean on september 25 1513 he saw it from the top of a mountain in what is now panama

2. alfred vail who helped develop morse code was born on this date in 1807

3. christopher columbus set sale on his second voyage to america on september 25 1493

4. benjamin harris published the first newspaper in america on this date in 1690

September 26

1. thomas jefferson was appointed the first secretary of state on september 26 1789

2. the federal trade commission was established on september 26 1914

3. john philip sousa performed his first concert on this date in 1895 he be none as a march composer

4. today is johnny appleseed day john johnny appleseed chapman was born on september 26 1775

September 27

1. edwin booth a famous american actor made his new york city debut on september 27 1850 fifteen years later edwins brother john would make headlines of his own what did john booth do

2. samuel adams a hero of the american revolution was born on september 27 1722

3. thomas nast a editorial cartoonist was born on this date in 1840

4. hiram rhodes revels was born on september 27 1822 he was the first african american senator he took office on febuary 25 1870

September 28

1. on september 28 1909 al capp was born he was the cartoonist and creater of lil abner

2. today is confucius birthday he was born in china nearly 2500 years ago he said what you do not wish for yourself do not do to others

3. president millard fillmore named brigham young the first governor of the territory of utah on september 28 1850

September 29

1. the first telephone message was sent across the u s on september 29 1915

2. enrico fermi a nobel prize winner in physics was born on this date in 1901

3. the bobbies of scotland yard made there first public appearance on september 29 1829

September 30

1. ether was first used as a anesthetic on september 30 1846

2. the first hydroelectric power station opened on this date in 1882

3. the tv cartoon the flintstones premiered on this day in 1960

October 1

1. james earl carter our thirty nine president was born on october 1 1924 the mideast peace treaty was signed in march of 1979 during president carters administration

2. the first game of the first world series ever played took place on october 1 1903

3. the first model t ford was introduced on october 1 1908

4. nigeria was proclaimed a independant nation on this date in 1960

October 2

1. on october 2 1872 jules verne introduced around the world in eighty days

2. mohandas k gandhi a indian pacifist was born on october 2 1869

3. the wild and scenic rivers act was passed on this date in 1968

4. robert h lawrence the first african american astronaut was born today in 1935

5. charlie brown and his friends was born on october 2 1950

October 3

1. on this day in 1863 president abraham lincoln declared thanksgiving a national holiday

2. thurgood marshall became the first african american supreme court justice on october 3 1967

3. william crawford gorgas was born on this date in 1854 he developed the cure for yellow fever

4. john thurman patented the first vacume cleaner on october 3 1899

October 4

1. saint francis of assisi was born on october 4 1181 or 1182 he and his followers formed the franciscan order of monks

2. president rutherford b hayes are nineteen presidant was born on this date in 1822

3. on october 4 1582 pope gregory 13 announced that the next day would not be october 5 but october 15 he changed the julian calender to the gregorian calender

October 5

1. president chester a arthur are twenty one presidant was born on october 5 1830

2. presidant harry s truman made the first presidential address telecast from the white house on this date in 1947

3. robert goddard was born on october 5 1882 this father of the space age was often ridiculed and ignored because he dreamed of rocket travel to other planets

October 6

1. george westinghouse inventer and manufacturer was born on october 6 1846

2. thomas a edison showed the first movie in west orange new jersey on this date in 1889

3. explorer and author thor heyerdahl was born on this date in 1914 he believed indians from south america might have settled the polynesian islands in 1947 he sailed a balsa wood raft from peru to polynesia to prove he might be write

October 7

1. on this date in 1986 president ronald reagan signed a bill which made the rose the national flower of the united states

2. james whitcomb riley righter of little orphan annie was born on october 7 1849

3. on october 7 1993 toni morrison became the first african american woman to win the nobel prize for literature.

October 8

1. civil rights leader jesse l jackson was born on october 8 1941

2. the great chicago fire beginned on october 8 1871 this fire left 300 people dead and 90000 without homes

3. on this date in 1871 a forest fire at peshtigo wisconsin burned sicks counties and killed more than 1100 people

4. on october 8 1945 paul robeson was awarded the spingarn medal for distinguished achievement in theater and concert

October 9

1. uganda was proclaimed a independant nation on october 9 1962

2. the finger print society was found on this date in 1915

3. today is leif ericson day this celebrates the discovery of north america about the year ad 1000 by leif ericson a norse explorer

4. the washington monument was opened to the public on october 9 1888 it is over 555 feet tall

October 10

1. the united states naval academy opened at annapolis on october 10 1845

2. martina navratilova a skilled tennis player was born in czechoslovakia on october 10 1956

3. vice presidant spiro t agnew who served under president richard nixon resigned from office on october 10 1973 due to charges of tax evasion

October 11

1. eleanor roosevelt wife of our thirty two presidant was born on october 11 1884 four many years she was a delegate to the united nations

2. apollo 7 the first manned apollo mission was sucessfully launched on october 11 1968

3. today is general casimir pulaski memorial day pulaski a hero of the revolutionary war died on this date in 1779

October 12

1. columbus cited san salvador island in central america on october 12 1492

2. elmer a sperry inventer of the gyrocompass was born on this date in 1860

3. on october 12 1960 soviet premier nikita khrushchev made an famous speech in front of the united nations assembly during the speech khrushchev pounded on a desk with a shoe to emphasize his point

October 13

1. the white house cornerstone was lade on october 13 1792

2. today is the birthday of the us navy its been in operation since 1775

3. football player jerry rice was born on october 13 1962 rice is generally considered to be the greatest wide receiver in professional football history

October 14

1. dwight david eisenhower our thirty fourth president was born on this date in 1890 ike had a successful military career prior to his presidency

2. william penn founder of the pennsylvania colony was born on october 14 1644

3. chuck yeager was the first human to break the sound barrier by flying the rocket powered bell x 1 airplane he did it on this date in 1947

4. on october 14 1066 william the conqueror and edward fought for the english crown at the battle of hastings william won

October 15

1. on this date in 1966 president lyndon johnson signed a bill which created the u s department of transportation

2. the tv show i love lucy premiered on october 15 1951

3. the first televised whether report took place on this date in 1953

October 16

1. on october 16 1859 john brown and his followers seized the federal arsenal in harpers ferry west virginia brown a white man who was executed for his actions fought to abolish slavery

2. today is dictionary day noah webster righter of the first american dictionary was born on october 16 1758

3. benjamin o davis sr becomed the first african american general in the regular army he did so on october 16 1940

4. today is national bosses day

October 17

1. general burgoyne surrendered at saratoga on october 17 1777

2. jupiter hammon was born on october 17 1711 he were the first african american to publish his own verse of poetry

3. shortly after 500 pm on october 17 1989 a large earth quake struck san francisco california collapsing a busy freeway and disrupting a world series game which was about to begin

October 18

1. on this date in 1968 american bob beamon set the world long jump record at the summer olympics in mexico city mexico

2. the mason dixon line was completed on october 18 1767

3. on this date in 1867 the american flag was raised at sitka in what is now known as alaska it had been purchased from russia for too cents a acre

October 19

1. its yorktown day in 1781 british general lord cornwallis and more than 7000 english and hessian soldiers surrendered to general george washington to end the war between britain and the colonies

2. president john adams was born on this date in 1735

3. thomas a edisons first successful demonstration of the electric light happened on october 19 1879

October 20

1. herbert clark hoover are thirty one presidant died on october 20 1964 his living could be characterised by calling him an humanitarian

2. john dewey a educator was born on october 20 1859

3. harold harris was the first to use a parachute after his plain became disabled it happened on october 20 1922

October 21

1. the uss constitution or old ironsides was launched on october 21 1797

2. on october 21 1520 magellan entered the straight that bares his name

3. alfred nobel was born on october 21 1833 this swedish inventers will has provided funds for the annual nobel prizes since 1901

October 22

1. the original new york metropolitan opera house opened on october 22 1883

2. sam houston was inaugurated as the first president of the republic of texas on october 22 1836

3. franz liszt was born on october 22 1811 this nineteenth century hungarian gave his first piano concert at the age of nine

October 23

1. this is the day when people in san juan capistrano california watch as the swallows leave for a winter home further south

2. talk show host johnny carson was born on october 23 1925

3. blanche scott became the first woman to fly solo in an airplane on this date in 1910

October 24

1. today is united nations day the charter for the united nations was signed today in 1945

2. sara josepha hale was born on october 24 1788 we have her to thank for are celebration of thanksgiving

3. the first transcontinental telegram was sent on this date in 1861 it traveled from san francisco california to new york city new york

October 25

1. the george washington bridge between new york and new jersey was opened on october 25 1931

2. pablo picasso one of the worlds greatest painters was born in spain on october 25 1881

3. richard evelyn byrd was born on october 25 1888 he devoted his live to aviation and poler exploration

October 26

1. on october 26 1994 beverly harvard became the first african american woman to be named chief of police on that day the city of atlanta georgia appointed her to the position

2. the erie canal opened on october 26 1825 it was the first major manmade waterway in the united states it extended from lake erie to the hudson river

3. the new york public libary opened it's doors on october 26 1911

October 27

1. the new york subway opened on this date in 1904 it was the first underwater and underground rail system ever built

2. presidant theodore roosevelt was born on october 27 1858 he was the first presidant to ride in a car submerge in a submarine and fly in a airplane

3. the first talking motion pitcher was shown to the public at warners theater in new york city on october 26 1927 al jolson had his screen debut in the jazz singer

October 28

1. the statue of liberty was dedicated by president grover cleveland on october 28 1886 some no it as liberty enlightening the world

2. during the dedication ceremony for the statue of liberty the first ticker tape parade took place

3. dr jonas salk was born on october 28 1914 he is responsible for the polio vaccination

4. terrell davis born on october 28 1972 was the mvp of super bowl xxxii which took place on january 25 1998 xxxii is the roman numeral version of what number

October 29

1. the stock market crashed on october 29 1929 this day known as black tuesday signaled the beginning of the great depression

2. edmund halley an astronomer who discovered a comet which is visible from earth every 76 years or so, was born on october 29 1656 look for halleys comet in the year 2062

3. the first trucking service started on october 29 1904 it hawled goods between colorado city colorado and snyder texas

October 30

1. john adams are second presidant was born on october 30 1735 his sun john quincy adams was our six president

2. on october 30 1938 a live radio program presented a play based on the book war of the worlds which described the invasion of earth by martians persons who tuned into the program late thought it was a real news broadcast and began to panic

3. ethel waters a actress and vocalist was born on october 30 1900

October 31

1. nevada became the thirty six state on october 31 1864

2. juliette gordon low founder of the girl scouts was born on october 31 1860

3. today is national magic day harry houdini the great escape artist died on october 31 1926

4. work on the massive sculpture on mount rushmore was completed on this day in 1941

November 1

1. election day for the presidency is the first tuesday after the first monday in november this takes place every four years

2. The white house become the official residents of the united states presidents on november 1 1800 john and abigail adams moved in on this date

3. the first issue of crisis was published by editor w e b dubois on november 1 1910

November 2

1. their was only twenty seven states in the union when are eleventh president james knox polk took office he was born on this date in 1795
2. november 2 1865 is the birth date of warren gamaliel harding he was born in corsica ohio and was our twenty nineth president
3. north dakota becomed the thirty nine state & south dakota becomed the forty state on november 2 1889
4. daniel boone the trailblazer of kentucky was born on this date in 1734
5. howard hughes spruce goose a huge airplane made of plywood made its first and only flight on november 2 1947 it was the worlds largest plain

November 3

1. today is sandwich day honoring the forth earl of sandwhich he were born today in england in 1718 and he invented the sandwich

2. the first automobile show opened in new york city at madison square garden on november 3 1900

3. panama gained its independance from colombia on november 3 1903 soon after the united states was granted permission to begin construction on the panama cannal

November 4

1. humorist will rogers was born on november 4 1879

2. the erie canal formally opened on november 4 1825

3. king tuts tomb was discovered on november 4 1922 by archeologist howard carter

4. the united states embassy personnel were taken hostage in iran on november 4 1979

November 5

1. the first colonial post office was established in boston massachusetts on november 5 1639

2. the first transcontinental flight was completed on november 5 1911

3. crossword puzzles were first published in book form on this date in 1924

4. shirley chisholm become the first african american women to be elected to the house of representatives she was elected on november 5 1958

November 6

1. today is adolphe sax birthday he was born on november 6 1814 he be the inventer of a musical instrument can you guess which one

2. john philip sousa march king and inventer of a musical instrument was born on november 6 1854

3. james naismith inventer of basketball was born on november 6 1861

4. the first intercollegiate football game in the united states was played on november 6 1869

November 7

1. on november 7 1811 general william henry harrison defeated indian attackers at the battle of tippecanoe

2. lewis and clarks expedition reached the pacific ocean on november 7 1805

3. the last spike was driven in the canadian pacific railway on november 7 1885

4. marie curie was born today in 1867 she was a french physicist who worked with her husband to research radioactivity

November 8

1. montana become the forty one state on november 8 1889 its capital is helena

2. the first circulating library was established by ben franklin in philadelphia on november 8 1731

3. margaret mitchell author of gone with the wind was born on november 8 1900

November 9

1. the holocaust beginned on november 9 1938 nazi storm troopers systematically burned synagogues luted jewish shops and began a era of persecution for all jews

2. benjamin banneker was born on november 9 1731 he was a engineer inventor mathematician and gazetteer

3. president theodore roosevelt sailed on a united states battleship for the panama canal zone he was the first president to leave the country while serving in office he set sail on november 9 1906

November 10

1. vincent van goghs irises sold for 53 point 9 million dollars on this date in 1987 making it the most expensive painting ever

2. the united states marine core was founded on november 10 1775

3. on november 10 1903 patent no 743801 was issued to mary anderson of massachusetts for the windshield wiper

November 11

1. washington become the forty two state on november 11 1889

2. today is veterans day we honor the man and woman who has served are country in the armed services

3. massachusetts passed the first compulsory school law on november 11 1647

November 12

1. auguste rodin a sculpter was borne on november 12 1840 his most famous sculpture is called the thinker

2. suffragist elizabeth cady stanton was born on november 12 1815 what is a suffragist

3. ellis island a united states immigration station closed on november 12 1954 it had been used as an detention & deportation center since 1891

November 13

1. the holland tunnel opened in new york city on november 13 1927

2. the holland tunnell connects canal street in manhattan new york to jersey city new jersey it consists of two tubes that are over 8000 feet in length

3. scottish author robert louis stevenson was born on november 13 1850 he wrote treasure island 1883 a childs garden of verses 1885 and several other classics

November 14

1. robert fulton inventer of the steamboat was born on november 14 1765 in lancaster county pennsylvania

2. claude monet a french painter was born on november 14 1840 he is famous for painting the same seen at different times of the day or year

3. on november 14 1969 three u s astronauts survived a launch aboard apollo 12 which saw them lose power temporarily power was restored and the mission was completed successfully

November 15

1. poet david mccord was born in new york city on november 15 1897

2. the articles of confederation was approved by congress on november 15 1777

3. pikes peak was discovered by zebulon pike on november 15 1806

4. today is shichi go san this japanese childrens festival is one of the most picturesque events of autumn parents thank the guardian spirits for the healthy growth of there children and prayers are offered for theyre further development

November 16

1. the first spacecraft to land on venus the soviet unions venera 3 was launched on this date in 1965

2. oklahoma was admitted to the union on november 16 1907

3. wc handy was born on november 16 1873 this american composer and bandleader was called the father of the blues

November 17

1. the suez canal opened on november 17 1869

2. lewis and clark reached the pasific ocean on november 17 1805

3. the infamous heidi game took place on this day in 1968 on that day the end of a televised football game was not seen by the viewing audience when the network decided to show the childrens program heidi instead the team which had been losing ended up winning in an exciting game

November 18

1. mickey mouse first appeared on the screen in steamboat willie on this date in 1929 it was shown at the colony theater in new york city it was the first animated talking picture

2. standard time begun in the united states on november 18 1883

3. louis daquerre father of photography was born today in 1789

4. the panama canal zone was created on november 18 1903

November 19

1. abraham lincoln delivered the gettysburg address on november 19 1863 he delivered his speech in too minutes how long is four score and seven years

2. president james a garfield are twenty presidant was born on november 19 1831 in orange ohio

3. george rogers clark a frontiersmen was born on november 19 1752

November 20

1. robert f kennedy was born on november 20 1925

2. robert f kennedy served as attorney general of the united states under his brother john f kennedy and was in the process of campaigning for the 1968 presidency when he was assassinated.

3. chester gould was born on november 20 1900 this popular cartoon artist created the dick tracy comic strip he drew and right it from its first appearance in 1931 until 1977

November 21

1. north carolina was the twelve state to ratify the constitution it did so on november 21 1789 it seceded on may 20 1861 and was re admitted in 1868

2. thomas a edison invented the phonograph on november 21 1877

3. the mayflower compact was signed on this date in 1620

4. baseball player ken griffey jr was born on november 21 1969 he and his father ken griffey sr were the first father and son duo to hit home runs for the same team in the same game in major league baseball history

November 22

1. our thirty five presidant john fitzgerald kennedy was assassinated on november 22 1963 he was the youngest president age 43 in our history he was also the youngest to die while in office he died at age 46

2. french explorer sieur de la salle was born on november 22 1643

3. sos was adopted as the international distress signal on november 22 1906

4. scientists at harvard university were the first to isolate the gene the basic unit of heredity they accomplished this feet on november 22 1969

November 23

1. franklin pierce was one of our youngest president's he became are forteen presidant at the age of 48 he was born on this date in 1804

2. henry mccarty was born on november 23 1859 he was better known as billy the kid

3. the female medical educational society of boston massachusetts was founded on november 23 1848

November 24

1. joseph f glidden received a patent for barbed wire on november 24 1874

2. president zachary taylor are twelve presidant was born on november 24 1784

3. carlo lorenzini author of pinocchio was born on this date in 1826

4. on november 24 1963 lee harvey oswald alleged assassin of president john f kennedy was shot by nightclub owner jack ruby this marked the first time a television audience viewed a murder as it was happening

5. scott joplin a pianist and composer was born on november 24 1868

November 25

1. on this day in 1963 president john f kennedy was buried in arlington national cemetery in arlington virginia arlington national cemetery which surrounds the former home of general robert e lee is also the burial site of william howard taft

2. andrew carnegie steel magnate and patron of libraries was born on november 25 1835

3. baseball star joe dimaggio was born on this date in 1914

November 26

1. the first streat railway in the united states began on november 26 1832

2. charles schulz creater of peanuts was born on this date in 1922

3. sojourner truth the first african american to speak out against slavery died on this date in 1883

4. casablanca starring humphrey bogart and ingrid bergman premiered on this day in 1942 on march 2 1944 it won the academy award for best picture of the year

November 27

1. thanksgiving day is the last thursday in november this tradition started in 1621 a year after the pilgrims' landed in the new world

2. magellan entered the pasific ocean on november 27 1520

3. the army war college was established on november 27 1901

4. inventive guitarist jimi hendrix was born on november 27 1942

November 28

1. william blake the english poet was born on november 28 1757 the tiger is won of his poems

2. the first united states post office opened in new york city on november 28 1785

3. richard wright the author of native son and black boy died on this date in 1960

November 29

1. admiral richard byrd flew over the south pole on november 29 1929

2. louisa may alcott author of such classics as little women was born on this date in 1832

3. bobby darins song mack the knife won the grammy award for best song on november 29 1959

November 30

1. samuel clemens was born on november 30 1835 his pen name is mark twain

2. jonathan swift author of gullivers travels was born on this date in 1667

3. winston churchill a english political leader was born on november 30 1874

December 1

1. on december 1 1955 rosa park's were arrested for refusing to relinquish her seet to a white passenger on a bus in montgomery alabama

2. woody allen was born on december 1 1935 he has written directed and starred in several famous films

3. hanukkah also known as the festival of lights lasts ate days it falls at the end of november or sometime during the month of december

December 2

1. the monroe doctrine was announced by president james monroe on december 2 1823 it stated that the united states foreign policy would be to seperate itself entirely from european influence

2. the first reindeer in the us was purchased from russia it arrive in alaska on december 2 1892

3. the first permanent artificial heart was implanted on december 2 1982

December 3

1. illinois becomed the twenty one state on december 3 1818

2. ellen henrietta richards founder of the home economics movement was born on december 3 1842

3. the first heart transplant which was performed by dr christian barnard took place in south africa on december 3 1967

December 4

1. the first man made satellite to orbit the planet venus was the pioneer venus 1 it began its orbit on december 4 1978

2. the amsterdam news the largest weakly community newspaper in the united states was founded on this date in 1909

3. the first agricultural society of importance in the us was founded on december 4 1867 it was called the grange

December 5

1. martin van buren our eight president was born on december 5 1782 before becoming president he was presidant jacksons secretary of state and later his vice president
2. walt disney producer of animated cartoons was born on december 5 1901
3. the montgomery bus boycott led by martin luther king jr began on this date in 1955
4. the twenty first amendment to the constitution was ratified on this day in 1933 this amendment repealed prohibition

December 6

1. joyce kilmer a poet was born on this date in 1886

2. on december 6 1933 a federal judge lifted a ban on the novel ulysses by james joyce when a work of art is banned because of its content that is called sensorship

3. its st nicholas day a day which honors a forth century bishop from partara turkey

December 7

1. delaware was the first state to ratify the united states constitution it did so on december 7 1787

2. president franklin d roosevelt proclaimed that december 7 1941 was a day that would live in infamy on that day japanese forces attacked pearl harbor in hawaii this event marked the official beginning of the united states involvement in world war ii

3. the first concert of the philharmonic symphony society of new york played on this date in 1842

December 8

1. the first greeting card designed by john calcott horsley was printed on december 8 1843

2. eli whitney inventer of the cotton gin was born on december 8 1765

3. on december 8 1980 former beatle john lennon was shot and killed outside of his new york city hotel by mark david chapman

December 9

1. clarence birdseye was born on december 9 1886 on a trip to labrador he noticed that quickly frozen fish were fresh and flavorful when thawed what food process do you think he started

2. tanzania was proclaimed a independant nation on this date in 1961

3. richard wrights novel native son was published on december 9 1940

December 10

1. swedish chemist alfred nobel the inventer of dynamite died on this date in 1896 money from his estate funds prizes for achievements in piece literature chemistry physics and medicine
2. martin luther king jr was awarded the nobel piece prize on this date in 1964
3. today is human rights day the un general assembly adopted the universal declaration of human rights this was done on december 10 1948
4. emily dickinson a poet was born today in 1830
5. mississippi became the twenty state on December 10 1817 it seceded in 1861 it was re admitted in 1870

December 11

1. the united nations international childrens emergency fund unicef was founded on this day in 1946

2. on december 11 1901 guglielmo marconi sent the first morse code radio signal across the alantic from england to newfoundland

3. indiana was admitted to the union on december 11 1816 it becomed the nineteen state

4. robert koch a german physician and bacteriologist was born on this date in 1843

December 12

1. today is poinsettia day dr j r poinsett who introduced the poinsettia to the united states from mexico died on this date in 1851

2. pennsylvania was the second state to ratify the constitution it did so on december 12 1787

3. kenya was proclaimed a independant nation on december 12 1963

4. washington dc became the official capitol of the united states on this date in 1800

December 13

1. the susan b anthony silver dollar was first coined on december 13 1978 it was the first u s coin to honor a woman

2. sir francis drake started a voyage around the world on december 13 1577

3. the clip-on tie was first designed on this day in 1928

December 14

1. on december 14 1819 alabama became the twenty two state to be admitted into the union it seceded on january 11 1861 and was re admitted in 1868

2. on december 14 1911 roald amundsen a norwegian explorer became the first person to reach the south pole

3. john mercer langston was won of the first african americans to be elected to public office he was born on december 14 1829

4. margaret chase smith was born on december 14 1897 she was the first women in the united states to serve in both the house of representatives and the senate

December 15

1. the first ten amendments the bill of rights was added to are constitution on december 15 1791

2. sitting bull a sioux indian leader died on this day in 1890

3. on december 15 1939 the movie gone with the wind premiered in atlanta georgia

December 16

1. tea anyone the boston tee party took place on december 16 1773

2. the germans begin the battle of the bulge on december 16 1944 during ww 2

3. composer ludwig van beethoven was born on december 16 1770

December 17

1. the first successful airplane flight took place on december 17 1903 today is right brothers day

2. peter shaffers amadeus a play about the life of composer wolfgang amadeus mozart opened in new york city on december 17 1980 the play later was made into a movie which won the academy award for best motion picture

3. on december 17 1933 the first national football league nfl championship game was played on that day the chicage bears won the new york giants by a score of 23 to 21

December 18

1. new jersey become the three state to ratify the constitution it did so on december 18 1787

2. the thirteen amendment to the us constitution which ended slavery was ratified on december 18 1865

3. joseph grimaldi has been called the greatest clown in history he was born on december 18 1778

December 19

1. walter williams the last living civil war veteran died on december 19 1959 he was 117 years old

2. the contintental army encamped at valley forge pennsylvania on december 19 1777 general washington was commander of the troops

3. anthropologist richard leakey was born today in 1944

4. the us satellite atlas broadcast the first radio voice from space on december 19 1958 it was a recorded christmas greating from president dwight d eisenhower

December 20

1. the louisiana purchase was made from france on december 20 1803 the united states purchased one million square miles four about 20 dollars per square mile

2. by this day in 1967 over 474000 u s troops had been sent to vietnam

3. on december 20 1977 president jimmy carter signed legislation which increased the social security tax

December 21

1. today is the first day of winter

2. today is forefathers day the pilgrims landed at plymouth rock massachusetts on december 21 1620

3. apollo 8 carrying the first humans to orbit the moon was launched on this date in 1968

4. on december 21 1956 the supreme courts decision ended the montgomery bus boycott with the integration of montgomery buses

December 22

1. the lincoln tunnel opened on december 22 1937 it linked new york to new jersey

2. colo was born at the columbus zoo on december 22 1956 she was the first gorilla born in captivity

3. radio city music hall located in new york cities rockefeller center opened on december 22 1932

December 23

1. on december 23 1975 the metric conversion act was adopted it made the metric system americas basic system of measurement

2. the us federal reserve system was extablished on december 23 1913

3. on this date in 1987 a plane landed in california after a journey of 24986 miles the plane had tooken off on december 14 and returned on this day after making a non stop flight around the world without refueling

December 24

1. frontiersmen scout and soilder kit carson was born on december 24 1809

2. general dwight d eisenhower was named supreme commander of allied forces on december 24 1943

3. december 24th is christmas eve for those who celebrate christmas certain christmas traditions such as decorating christmas trees and mailing christmas cards did not become popular customs until the 1800s

December 25

1. sir isaac newton was born on december 25 1642

2. mikhail gorbachev resigned as leader of the soviet union on december 25 1991 the soviet union dissolved into independent countries soon after this event

3. clara barton founder of the american red cross was born on december 25 1821

December 26

1. while british troops quartered in philadelphia george washington led his army across the deleware river to new jersey on december 25 1776 he took 1400 hessian soldiers by surprise early on december 26

2. today is the first day of kwanzaa first fruit this african american family observance has been held since 1966 its a recognition of african harvest festivals

3. baseball player ozzie smith was born on december 26 1954 he is known for his incredible defense

December 27

1. what do pasteurization vaccination and the rabies vaccine have in common all where invented or developed by louis pasteur a french biochemist he was born on december 27 1822

2. sir george cayley was born on december 27 1773 he is considered to be the father of aerodynamics

3. apollo 8 returned to earth on december 27 1968 during its mission the apollo 8 orbited the moon ten times

December 28

1. woodrow wilson are twenty eight president was born on december 28 1856

2. iowa was admitted as the twenty nine state on december 28 1846

3. w f semple recieved the first patent for chewing gum he did so on december 28 1869

4. a penny saved is a penny earned benjamin franklin made that statement he beginned publishing poor richards almanack on this date in 1732

December 29

1. texas was admitted as the twenty eight state on december 29 1845 it seceded from the union on january 28 1861 and was re admitted in 1870

2. president andrew johnson are seventeen president was born on this date in 1808

3. the first ymca in the us was founded on december 29 1851

4. pablo casals was born in spain on december 29 1876 he was a master cello player

December 30

1. rudyard kipling a english poet and righter of jungle book was born on december 30 1865

2. the first free way in california opened on december 30 1940 it connected los angeles to pasadena

3. golfer tiger woods was born on december 30 1975

December 31

1. ellis island opened on december 31 1890 as a us port of entry for emmigrants

2. baseball great roberto clemente died in a plane crash on december 31 1972 while flying supplies for earthquake relief to nicaragua he ended his career with exactly 3000 hits

3. hulan jack became borough president of manhattan on december 31 1953 he was the first african american to hold a major elective office in a major american city

4. happy new year

Calendar Grids

January

Sun	Mon	Tue	Wed	Thu	Fri	Sat

February

Sun	Mon	Tue	Wed	Thu	Fri	Sat

Calendar Grids *(cont.)*

March

Sun	Mon	Tue	Wed	Thu	Fri	Sat

April

Sun	Mon	Tue	Wed	Thu	Fri	Sat

Calendar Grids *(cont.)*

May

Sun	Mon	Tue	Wed	Thu	Fri	Sat

June

Sun	Mon	Tue	Wed	Thu	Fri	Sat

Calendar Grids *(cont.)*

July

Sun	Mon	Tue	Wed	Thu	Fri	Sat

August

Sun	Mon	Tue	Wed	Thu	Fri	Sat

Calendar Grids *(cont.)*

September

Sun	Mon	Tue	Wed	Thu	Fri	Sat

October

Sun	Mon	Tue	Wed	Thu	Fri	Sat

Calendar Grids *(cont.)*

November

Sun	Mon	Tue	Wed	Thu	Fri	Sat

December

Sun	Mon	Tue	Wed	Thu	Fri	Sat

Answer Key

January 1
1. Sudan was proclaimed an independent nation on January 1, 1956. Sudan is on the continent of Africa.
2. The laws outlined in the Emancipation Proclamation went into effect on January 1, 1863. It was signed by President Abraham Lincoln.
3. Great Americans Betsy Ross, flagmaker, and Paul Revere, soldier and patriot, were born on this date. Ross was born in 1752. Revere was born in 1735.
4. In Pasadena, CA, the Tournament of Roses, has taken place on this date since 1886.

January 2
1. The first commemorative postage stamp was issued by the United States Post Office Department on January 2, 1893.
2. Georgia became a state in 1776. It was the fourth state to ratify the Constitution. It did so on January 2, 1788. It seceded on January 19, 1861, and was readmitted on July 15, 1870.
3. Today is National Science Fiction Day. Isaac Asimov, a famous science fiction writer, was born on this day in 1920.

January 3
1. Alaska is the largest state in the United States. It is more than twice the size of Texas. Alaska entered the Union on January 3, 1959. It is our forty-ninth state.
2. The March of Dimes was established on January 3, 1938, to raise funds for polio research.
3. Lucretia Coffin Mott, a women's rights advocate, was born on January 3, 1793.
4. The Battle of Princeton took place on January 3, 1777.

January 4
1. Louis Braille, inventor of the Braille alphabet system for the blind, was born on this date in 1809.
2. English scientist Sir Isaac Newton, discoverer of the law of gravity, was born on January 4, 1642.
3. Utah became the forty-fifth state on January 4, 1896.
4. Jacob Grimm, author of fairy tales, was born on January 4, 1785.

January 5
1. Nellie Tayloe Ross became the first woman governor in the United States. She became governor of Wyoming on January 5, 1925.
2. The Great Northern Railway was completed on January 5, 1893.
3. Today is Bird Day! The National Audubon Society was founded in 1905.
4. Stephen Decatur, a United States naval hero, was born on January 5, 1779.

January 6
1. New Mexico became the 47th state on this day in 1912.
2. Carl Sandburg, a poet and author, was born on January 6, 1878.
3. Pan American Airways achieved the first around-the-world commercial flight on January 6, 1942.
4. George Washington Carver was born a slave on January 6, 1864, in Diamond Grove, Missouri.

January 7
1. President Millard Fillmore was born on January 7, 1800. He was our thirteenth president. He belonged to the Whig political party.
2. Transatlantic telephone service began on January 7, 1927.
3. The first national election in the United States took place on January 7, 1789.
4. The first United States commercial bank opened in Philadelphia on January 7, 1782.

January 8
1. Rock 'n' roll performer Elvis Presley was born on January 8, 1935.
2. Andrew Jackson defeated the British at the Battle of New Orleans on January 8, 1815.
3. President Washington delivered the first State of the Union address on January 8, 1790.

January 9
1. President Richard Nixon, our thirty-seventh president, was born on January 9, 1913.
2. The Seeing Eye organization was incorporated on January 9, 1929. It trains dogs to guide the blind. The organization is located in Morristown, New Jersey.
3. Carrie Chapman Catt, a women's suffrage leader, was born on January 9, 1859.
4. The first United States balloon flight happened on January 9, 1793.

Answer Key (cont.)

January 10
1. Ethan Allen, leader of the Green Mountain Boys, was born on January 10, 1738.
2. The first oil strike in Texas happened on January 10, 1901.
3. The first session of the United Nations took place on January 10, 1946.
4. The first racial integration of public education in Georgia happened on January 10, 1961.

January 11
1. Alexander Hamilton, the first secretary of the United States Treasury, was born on January 11, 1757.
2. On this day in 1964, U.S. Surgeon General Luther Terry issued the first government warning stating that smoking may be hazardous to a person's health.
3. Philosopher William James was born on January 11, 1842. He said that people "only use 10% of their minds."

January 12
1. Playwright Lorraine Hansberry, who wrote *A Raisin in the Sun*, died on January 12, 1965.
2. Fairy tale writer Charles Perrault was born on January 12, 1628. He wrote *Sleeping Beauty, Little Red Riding Hood*, and *Cinderella*.
3. The first public museum was founded in Charleston, South Carolina, on January 12, 1773.

January 13
1. Stephen Foster died on this day in 1864. He wrote the songs "Oh, Susanna" and "Camptown Races."
2. The accordion was patented on January 13, 1854.
3. Horatio Alger, a novelist, was born on January 13, 1834.
4. The first public radio broadcast took place on this day in 1910. It featured several opera singers.

January 14
1. The Simpsons, an animated TV series, premiered on January 14, 1990.
2. Born in England on January 14, 1886, Hugh Lofting wrote many books, including his *Doctor Doolittle* series.
3. Albert Schweitzer, a humanitarian, was born on January 14, 1875.

4. American officer Benedict Arnold was born on this date in 1741. He deserted to the British during the Revolutionary War.

January 15
1. Martin Luther King, Jr., leader of the nonviolent civil rights movement in the United States in the '60s, was born in Atlanta, Georgia, on January 15, 1929.
2. The first annual Super Bowl was played on January 15, 1967. On that day, the Green Bay Packers beat the Kansas City Chiefs, 35–10.
3. Mathew B. Brady, the first photographer to record Civil War battlefields, died on January 15, 1896.

January 16
1. Robert Service, a poet, was born on January 16, 1874.
2. The Civil Service system was established on January 16, 1883.
3. The U.S. National Aeronautics and Space Administration (NASA) accepted its first women candidates for astronauts on January 16, 1978.

January 17
1. Rutherford Birchard Hayes, our nineteenth president, died on January 17, 1822. He was born in Delaware, Ohio. After retiring from the presidency, he lived in Fremont, Ohio.
2. Happy Birthday, Ben! Benjamin Franklin, a scientist and statesman, was born on January 17, 1706.
3. Prizefighter Muhammed Ali was born on January 17, 1942, in Louisville, Kentucky. His given name was Cassius Clay.

January 18
1. Daniel Webster, a statesman, was born on January 18, 1782.
2. A. A. Milne, author of the *Winnie-the-Pooh* books, was born on January 18, 1882.
3. Peter Roget was born on January 18, 1779. His name is synonymous with the thesaurus.

January 19
1. Confederate General Robert E. Lee was born on January 19, 1807.
2. James Watt, inventor of steam power, was born on this date in 1736.

Answer Key (cont.)

3. Edgar Allan Poe was born on January 19, 1809. He wrote many famous tales of horror.

January 20

1. Congress ratified the Twentieth Amendment to the Constitution in 1933. It stated that a president's term of office would begin on January 20th, rather than March 4th.
2. The main event of inauguration day, the day the new president takes the oath of office, occurs at noon on January 20th on the Capitol steps in Washington, D.C.
3. On January 20, 1981, the same day that Ronald Reagan was inaugurated as president of the United States, the Iranian hostage crisis ended and 52 American captives were released.

January 21

1. *Nautilus*, the first atomic-powered ship, was launched on January 21, 1954. It was the first ship to reach the North Pole. It did so on August 3, 1958.
2. Confederate General Stonewall Jackson was born on January 21, 1824.
3. The first novel published in America was published on this day in 1789.

January 22

1. The first postal route, which was from Boston to New York, was established on January 22, 1672.
2. Andre Ampere was born on January 22, 1775. The ampere, the unit of electrical current, was named after him.
3. A Vietnam War peace agreement was signed on January 22, 1973. It called for a cease-fire throughout North and South Vietnam.

January 23

1. John Hancock was born today in 1737. He was the first man to sign the Declaration of Independence.
2. The U.S. Navy bathysphere, *Trieste*, went 24,000 feet to the bottom of Mariana Trench in the Pacific Ocean on January 23, 1960.
3. Althea Gibson became the first African American voted Female Athlete of the Year. It happened on January 23, 1958.

January 24

1. Maria Tallchief, an American ballerina, was born on January 24, 1925.

2. John Sutter found gold in Sacramento Valley, California, on January 24, 1848.
3. On January 24, 1962, Jackie Robinson became the first African American elected to the National Baseball Hall of Fame.
4. The first ice-cream bar, the Eskimo Pie, was patented on this day in 1922.

January 25

1. On January 25, 1998, John Elway led the Denver Broncos in their victory over the Green Bay Packers. The win was the Broncos' first in five attempts since 1978.
2. The first transcontinental telephone call took place on January 25, 1915. It was placed between San Francisco and New York.
3. On January 25, 1961, President John F. Kennedy held the first televised presidential news conference.

January 26

1. Michigan became the twenty-sixth state on January 26, 1837.
2. General Douglas MacArthur was born on January 26, 1880.
3. On January 26, 1961, hockey player Wayne Gretzky was born.
4. Australia, the world's only country-continent, was first settled by colonists on January 26, 1788.

January 27

1. Wolfgang Amadeus Mozart was born on January 27, 1756.
2. Lewis Carroll (Charles Dodgson), author of *Alice in Wonderland*, was born on this date in 1832.
3. Today is the anniversary of the official signing of a peace agreement ending the Vietnam War. The agreement was reached in 1973.
4. Three *Apollo I* astronauts were killed in a fire during ground testing on January 27, 1967.

January 28

1. South Carolina and six other states seceded from the United States on January 28, 1861. They called themselves the Confederate States of America and named Jefferson Davis their leader.
2. Sir Francis Drake, an English explorer, was born on this date in 1540.

Answer Key *(cont.)*

3. On January 28, 1986, seven astronauts were killed in the *Challenger* explosion at the Kennedy Space Center in Florida.
4. The U.S. Coast Guard was established on January 28, 1915.

January 29
1. Our twenty-fifth president, William McKinley, was born on January 29, 1843, in Niles, Ohio. He was assassinated by Leon Czolgosz. He was one of our most-loved presidents.
2. Kansas became the thirty-fourth state on January 29, 1861.
3. Thomas Paine, a Revolutionary War patriot and writer, was born on January 29, 1737.

January 30
1. Franklin Delano Roosevelt was born on this date in 1882. He is the only president to be elected to four terms. He was our thirty-second president.
2. The Baseball Hall of Fame was established on January 30, 1936.
3. Mahatma Gandhi was assassinated on January 30, 1948. Gandhi didn't believe in using violence to achieve one's goals.

January 31
1. The United States launched its first satellite, *Explorer I*, on January 31, 1958.
2. Several great major league baseball players were born on January 31. Jackie Robinson, most known for breaking the color barrier in baseball, was born on January 31, 1919. Also, Ernie Banks, whose nickname was "Mr. Cub," was born on this date in 1931, and Nolan Ryan, the all-time strikeout king, was born on January 31, 1947.
3. The first McDonald's restaurant in the Soviet Union opened on this day in 1990.

February 1
1. Today is Robinson Crusoe Day! Alexander Selkirk, the Scottish sailor who became the model for Daniel Defoe's *Robinson Crusoe*, was rescued from the Juan Fernandez Islands on February 1, 1709.
2. Langston Hughes, a poet, was born on February 1, 1902.
3. Julia Ward Howe's "Battle Hymn of the Republic" was published on February 1, 1862.

February 2
1. Happy Groundhog Day! Did the groundhog see his shadow? If so, it's six more weeks of winter.
2. Irish novelist James Joyce was born on February 2, 1882.
3. On February 2, 1935, the first lie detector test was taken.

February 3
1. Elizabeth Blackwell was born on February 3, 1821. In 1849 she became the first American woman to receive a degree as a medical doctor.
2. Norman Rockwell, a popular American painter, was born on February 3, 1884.
3. The Fifteenth Amendment to the U.S. Constitution granted all citizens the right to vote and was ratified on February 3, 1870.

February 4
1. Charles A. Lindbergh, an aviator, was born on February 4, 1902. He was the first person to fly across the Atlantic Ocean alone. He became known as "Lucky Lindy."
2. Rosa Parks, mother of the modern Civil Rights movement, was born on February 4, 1913.
3. The Confederate States of America was founded in Alabama on February 4, 1861.

February 5
1. Roger Williams, founder of Rhode Island, arrived in America on February 5, 1631.
2. Hank Aaron was born on February 5, 1934. He became the all-time home run king when he hit his 715th home run in 1974. He broke the record of Babe Ruth.
3. The longest war in history ended on February 5, 1985. The Third Punic War began in 149 B.C. and lasted 2,131 years!

February 6
1. Ronald Reagan, our fortieth president, was born on February 6, 1911. He was the oldest man ever elected as president (age 69 in '80, 73 in '84).
2. Massachusetts became the sixth state to ratify the Constitution. It did so on February 6, 1788.
3. George Herman "Babe" Ruth was born on February 6, 1895. He hit 714 home runs during his career. He hit many of his home runs in Yankee Stadium. It became known as "The House That Ruth Built."

Answer Key *(cont.)*

February 7

1. Frederick Douglass, an escaped slave who became a leading abolitionist, was born on February 7, 1817.
2. Charles Dickens, an English novelist, was born on this date in 1812.
3. Sinclair Lewis, a novelist, was born on February 7, 1885.
4. Laura Ingalls Wilder was born on this day in 1867. She began writing the *Little House* books when she was sixty-five years old.

February 8

1. The Boy Scouts of America was founded on February 8, 1910.
2. On February 8, 1735, the first opera in the American colonies was performed.
3. Writer Jules Verne was born on February 8, 1823. *Twenty Thousand Leagues Under the Sea* and *Around the World in Eighty Days* were published in 1873. These books are still popular today.
4. Actor James Dean was born on this day in 1931.

February 9

1. The United States Weather Service was established on February 9, 1870.
2. William Henry Harrison, our ninth president, was born on February 9, 1773.
3. On February 9, 1909, the first school to give scientific training in the care and preservation of shade trees was founded.

February 10

1. The first singing telegram was sent on February 10, 1933.
2. Samuel Plimsoll, born on February 10, 1824, was upset about the overloading of cargo ships. He worked to pass laws limiting how much could be put on ships.
3. Olympic swimmer Mark Spitz was born in Modesto, California, on February 10, 1950. He set a world record at the 1972 Olympic Games in Munich, Germany, by winning seven gold medals.

February 11

1. Thomas Alva Edison was born on February 11, 1847. Edison said that "genius is 1% inspiration and 99% perspiration."
2. Today is National Inventors Day!
3. The first hospital in America opened in Philadelphia on February 11, 1751.

Benjamin Franklin and Dr. Thomas Hood worked to established this hospital.

February 12

1. Abraham Lincoln was born on February 12, 1809. He was our sixteenth president. We celebrate President's Day the third Monday in February to honor President Washington and President Lincoln.
2. The National Association for the Advancement of Colored People (NAACP) was founded on this date in 1909.
3. Thaddeus Kosciusko, a Polish patriot and aide to General Washington, was born on February 12, 1746.
4. Charles Darwin was born in Shrewsbury, England, on February 12, 1809.

February 13

1. Boston Latin Grammar School, the oldest public school still in existence in the United States, began on February 13, 1635.
2. Grant Wood, an American primitive painter, was born on February 13, 1892.
3. The first magazine published in America, *The American Magazine* was presented on February 13, 1741.

February 14

1. Arizona became the forty-eighth state on February 14, 1912.
2. Oregon became the thirty-third state on February 14, 1859.
3. Today is Valentine's Day!
4. G. W. Gale Ferris was born on February 14, 1859. What amusement park ride do you suppose he introduced?

February 15

1. Cyrus McCormick, an inventor, was born on February 15, 1809.
2. Galileo Galilei, an Italian astronomer and mathematician, was born on this date in 1564.
3. Susan B. Anthony, a crusader for women's rights, was born on February 15, 1820.
4. Charles Tiffany, born on this date in 1812, is known for his jewelry designs and jewelry store. His son, Louis Tiffany, born on February 18, 1848, is known for his intricate artwork of stained glass.

February 16

1. Henry Adams, a historian, was born on February 16, 1838.

Answer Key *(cont.)*

2. On February 16, 1960, the submarine *Triton* left New London, Connecticut, on a trip around the world. It returned on May 11.
3. Yonge Street in Toronto, Canada, is the world's longest street. It opened on February 16, 1796.

February 17

1. Today is PTA Founders Day. The National Congress of Parents and Teachers was founded on February 17, 1897.
2. The War of 1812 ended on February 17, 1815.
3. Marian Anderson, a contralto singer, was born on February 17, 1902.
4. Basketball star Michael Jordan was born February 17, 1963.

February 18

1. San Francisco's Golden Gate International Exposition opened on February 18, 1939.
2. Clyde W. Tombaugh discovered our farthest planet, Pluto, on February 18, 1930. Pluto is the outermost of the nine planets in our solar system.
3. Mark Twain's *The Adventures of Huckleberry Finn* was published on this day in 1885.

February 19

1. Thomas Edison patented the phonograph on this day in 1878.
2. Nicolaus Copernicus, an astronomer of Polish descent, was born on February 19, 1473. He founded modern astronomy around 1543. He discovered that Earth is a moving planet and the sun is the center of the solar system.
3. The manufacturers of Cracker Jacks began including a prize in each box on this day in 1913.

February 20

1. On February 20, 1962, Lieutenant Colonel John Glenn, Jr., became the first American to orbit Earth.
2. The United States purchased the Virgin Islands from Denmark on February 20, 1917.
3. Today in 1872, the Metropolitan Museum of Art opened in New York City.
4. Frederick Douglass died on February 20, 1895. He was born a slave in Tuckahoe, Maryland. He gained his freedom by escaping from his master.

February 21

1. The Washington Monument, built in honor of our first president, was dedicated on February 21, 1885.
2. On February 21, 1878, the first telephone directory was issued in New Haven, Connecticut.
3. On February 21, 1972, Richard Nixon became the first U.S. president to visit China.

February 22

1. George Washington was born on this date in 1732. He was our first president.
2. Frank W. Woolworth opened his first 5-cent store on February 22, 1879.
3. On this day in 1924, President Calvin Coolidge made the first public radio broadcast from the White House.

February 23

1. John Quincy Adams, our sixth president and the son of our second president, died on this date in 1848.
2. The Marines raised the United States flag on Mt. Suribachi, Iwo Jima, on February 23, 1945. This took place after a battle during World War II. A photographer took their picture and won a Pulitzer Prize.
3. George Frederick Handel was born on February 23, 1685. He is considered one of the greatest musicians of all time.

February 24

1. Pope Gregory XIII established the modern calendar on February 24, 1582.
2. The first rocket to reach outer space blasted off from White Sands Proving Grounds, New Mexico, on this date in 1949. This two-stage rocket reached an altitude of 250 miles.

February 25

1. The income tax law was adopted on February 25, 1913, with the passing of the Sixteenth Amendment.
2. Francisco Coronado embarked upon the exploration of Mexico and the southwestern United States on this date in 1540.
3. The first Timberland Protection Act was passed by Congress on February 25, 1779.
4. Adelle Davis, an American nutritionist and author, was born on February 25, 1905. Her message was, "You are what you eat."

Answer Key *(cont.)*

5. Hiram Rhodes Revels was the first African American to take office as a United States Senator. He did so on February 25, 1870.

February 26
1. William "Buffalo Bill" Cody was born on February 26, 1846.
2. The first around-the-world nonstop airplane flight took off from Fort Worth, Texas, on February 26, 1949.
3. Levi Strauss was born on this date in 1829. He is the inventor of blue jeans.
4. Congress established the Grand Canyon in Arizona as a national park on February 26, 1919.

February 27
1. Henry Wadsworth Longfellow, a poet, was born on February 27, 1807. One of his popular poems is called "The Song of Hiawatha."
2. Voting by women was declared legal by the Supreme Court on this date in 1922.
3. The Twenty-second Amendment to the Constitution was ratified on this date in 1951. It stated that "no person shall be elected to the office of the president more than twice."
4. The Gulf War ended on February 27, 1991, forty days after it had begun.

February 28
1. The Republican Party was organized on February 28, 1854.
2. The final episode of *M*A*S*H* aired on this day in 1983. This event was the most-watched series TV show ever.
3. Vaslav Nijinsky, a famous ballet dancer, was born on February 28, 1890. He was born in Kiev, Russia.

February 29
1. Leap year happens every four years. This extra day is added to make our calendar year more nearly match the solar system.
2. On this day in 1940, *Gone with the Wind* won the Academy Award for Best Motion Picture of 1939. One member of the film's cast, Hattie McDaniel, became the first African-American actress to win an Oscar.

March 1
1. Ohio became the United States' seventeenth state on March 1, 1803. President Thomas Jefferson was president at that time. Its capital is Columbus.
2. Nebraska became the thirty-seventh state on March 1, 1867.
3. Yellowstone became the first national park in the United States on March 1, 1872. It was established in Idaho, Wyoming, and Montana.
4. The first United States census was authorized by Congress on this date in 1790. The results: Virginia was the most populated state, and Philadelphia, Pennsylvania, was the most populated American city.
5. On March 1, 1780, Pennsylvania became the first state to officially abolish slavery.

March 2
1. Wilt Chamberlain, a basketball star, scored one hundred points against the New York Knickerbockers on March 2, 1962.
2. Theodore Seuss Geisel (Dr. Seuss) was born on March 2, 1904.
3. Sam Houston, a frontiersman, was born on this date in 1793.
4. Today is National Teacher's Day! Have you hugged your teacher today?

March 3
1. Florida became the twenty-seventh state on March 3, 1845. It seceded in 1861 and was readmitted in 1868.
2. On March 3, 1931, President Hoover signed a bill making "The Star-Spangled Banner" the national anthem.
3. The adhesive postage stamp was first approved by Congress on this date in 1847.
4. Alexander Graham Bell, inventor of the telephone, was born on March 3, 1847.

March 4
1. Vermont joined the Union as the fourteenth state on March 4, 1791.
2. Today is Constitution Day. The United States Constitution went into effect on March 4, 1789.
3. Garrett Morgan, inventor of the gas inhaler and traffic signal, was born today in 1877.
4. The United States Congress created the Department of Labor on March 4, 1913. The department's purpose is to protect the welfare of workers in the United States.

March 5
1. Gerald Mercator, a Flemish mapmaker, was born on March 5, 1512.

Answer Key *(cont.)*

2. The first bloodshed of the American Revolution took place on this date in 1770. It's known as the Boston Massacre.
3. Today is Crispus Attucks Day. On March 5, 1770, this black member of a group of Boston patriots was the first person to die in the Boston Massacre.

March 6
1. On March 6, 1836, the Alamo was captured. After holding out for nearly two weeks, Texans fortified in the Alamo were killed by the Mexican General Santa Ana.
2. Michelangelo Buonarroti, an Italian artist, was born on this date in 1475. He painted the ceiling of the Sistine Chapel and is considered one of the world's greatest artists.
3. The United States Bureau of Census was established on March 6, 1902.
4. Ghana became an independent nation on March 6, 1957.

March 7
1. Luther Burbank, a botanist and horticulturist, was born on this date in 1849.
2. Victor Farris, inventor, industrialist, and multimillionaire, died on March 7, 1985. Of the 200 patents he owned, his best known patent is probably the paper milk carton.
3. Alexander Graham Bell patented the telephone on March 7, 1876.

March 8
1. The first American combat troops arrived in Vietnam on March 8, 1965.
2. On March 8, 1945, Phyllis Mae Daley became the first African-American woman to be commissioned in the Navy Nurse Corps.
3. Oliver Wendell Holmes, Jr., a Supreme Court justice, was born on March 8, 1841.
4. Today is International Women's Day!

March 9
1. The battle between the *Monitor* and *Merrimack* took place on March 9, 1862. It was a famous sea battle during the Civil War.
2. Amerigo Vespucci was born on March 9, 1454. He was an explorer.

3. Richard Adams died today in 1988. Adams invented the paint roller during World War II when there was a shortage of paintbrushes.
4. The first patent for artificial teeth was granted on March 9, 1822.

March 10
1. The first words ever spoken over the telephone happened on this date in 1876.
2. The Salvation Army started in the United States on March 10, 1880.
3. Today is Harriet Tubman Day. She was born into slavery in Dorchester County, Maryland. She died on March 10, 1913. She's buried in Ohio.

March 11
1. The first snowfall in the famous blizzard of 1888 took place on March 11th. By the time it quit, 40 to 50 inches of snow had fallen.
2. John Chapman (Johnny Appleseed), a frontier hero and horticulturist, died on March 11, 1845.
3. Lorraine Hansberry's *A Raisin in the Sun* became the first play by an African-American woman to premiere on Broadway. It did so on March 11, 1959.

March 12
1. The Girl Scouts of America were founded on March 12, 1912.
2. The United States Post Office Department was established on this date in 1789.
3. Charlie "Bird" Parker, a genius of modern jazz, died on March 12, 1955.
4. American author Jack Kerouac was born on March 12, 1922. His most famous book is called *On the Road*.
5. Charles Boycott, born today in 1832, left his name to the English language. After he issued eviction notices to his tenants, they refused to have anything to do with him.

March 13
1. Chester Greenwood patented the first earmuffs on March 13, 1877.
2. Chicago was founded by Jean Baptiste Pointe du Sable on March 13, 1773.
3. One of the discoverers of oxygen was Joseph Priestley. He was born on March 13, 1733.

Answer Key *(cont.)*

4. The planet Uranus was discovered by astronomer William Herschel on this day in 1781.

March 14

1. Albert Einstein, a mathematician and physicist, was born on March 14, 1879. He is best known for his theory of relativity.
2. Eli Whitney patented the cotton gin on this date in 1794.
3. Baseball great Kirby Puckett was born on March 14, 1961.

March 15

1. Andrew Jackson was born on this date in 1767. He was our seventh president and was the first to represent the plain, common people instead of the rich.
2. Maine became the twenty-third state on March 15, 1820.
3. The people of Hinckley, Ohio, begin to look for buzzards to arrive today. These birds will begin to build their nests.
4. Julius Caesar was assassinated on this day in 44 B.C.

March 16

1. Today is our fourth president's birthday. James Madison was born in 1751. He created the Constitution and fought for the addition of the first ten amendments known as the "Bill of Rights."
2. The United States Military Academy was established on March 16, 1802.
3. Comedian Jerry Lewis, born on March 16, 1926, is remembered most for his Labor Day telethon to raise money for muscular dystrophy.
4. On March 16, 1960, San Antonio, Texas, became the first major southern city to integrate lunch counters.

March 17

1. Singer Nat King Cole was born in Montgomery, Alabama, on March 17, 1919.
2. The Camp Fire Girls was founded on this date in 1910.
3. Today is St. Patrick's Day! One of the most popular legends is that St. Patrick drove all the snakes out of Ireland and into the sea. Did you know that the shamrock is the national flower of Ireland? Check your encyclopedia for more information.

March 18

1. Happy Birthday, Grover Cleveland! You were the only president to serve two terms out of sequence. You were our twenty-second and twenty-fourth president. You were born today in 1837.
2. Statehood was granted to Hawaii on March 18, 1959.
3. Rudolph Diesel, born March 18, 1858, was a German engineer and inventor of an engine that bears his name.
4. Holbert Rillieux, an African-American scientist, was born on March 18, 1806. He revolutionized the sugar industry.

March 19

1. Today the cliff swallows make their annual journey from Argentina to San Juan Capistrano, California.
2. When Congress passed the Standard Time Act on March 19, 1918, it established daylight-saving time.
3. Ptolemy, an astronomer, recorded the first eclipse of the moon on this day in 72 A.D.

March 20

1. *Uncle Tom's Cabin*, by Harriet Beecher Stowe, was published on March 20, 1852.
2. Fred Rogers was born today in 1928. His television show, *Mister Rogers' Neighborhood*, has been a favorite for young children since 1965.
3. Sir Isaac Newton died on March 20, 1727, in Kensington, England.

March 21

1. Today is the traditional date for the beginning of spring.
2. Benito Juarez was born on March 21, 1806. He is considered the "George Washington of Mexico."
3. Cesar Chavez was born on March 21, 1927. He's known for his work for better conditions for Mexican-American farm workers in the Southwest.
4. Artist Randolph Caldecott was born in Chester, England, on March 21, 1846. The Caldecott Medal is named for this artist.

March 22

1. The United States granted independence to the Philippines on March 22, 1934.

Answer Key *(cont.)*

2. Marcel Marceau, born today in 1923, is an actor who does pantomime.
3. Arthur Schawlow and Charles Townes patented the first laser on March 22, 1960.

March 23

1. Patrick Henry gave his famous speech, "Give Me Liberty or Give Me Death," on March 23, 1775.
2. Roger Bannister was born on March 23, 1929. In 1954 he officially became the first person to run a mile in less than four minutes.
3. Elisha Graves Otis installed the first passenger elevator in the United States on March 23, 1857.
4. The first standing ovation was given on this day in 1743. King George stood to applaud a performance of Handel's *Messiah,* and others followed his lead.

March 24

1. Robert Koch announced the discovery of the tuberculosis germ on March 24, 1882.
2. Today is Agriculture Day.
3. The first white man to explore the Grand Canyon from the bottom was geologist John Wesley Powell. He was born on March 24, 1834.
4. One of the greatest man-made disasters ever occurred on this day in 1989 when the Exxon *Valdez* oil tanker spilled over 11,000,000 gallons of its cargo off the coast of Alaska.

March 25

1. Lord Baltimore's colonists landed in Maryland on March 25, 1634.
2. On March 25, 1965, Viola Liuzzo, a 39-year-old, white Civil Rights worker from Detroit, was shot and killed by Klan members on Highway 80 near Montgomery, Alabama.
3. Singer and songwriter Aretha Franklin was born today in 1942. She has received Grammy awards for her rhythm-and-blues records and for her soul/gospel performances.
4. Gutzon Borglum, an African sculptor, was born on March 25, 1871. He is best known for the Mount Rushmore Memorial in South Dakota.

March 26

1. Robert Frost, a poet, was born on March 26, 1874.
2. Sandra Day O'Connor was born on March 26, 1930. She was sworn in as an associate judge of the U.S. Supreme Court on September 25, 1981. She is the first woman ever appointed to this high court.
3. The lifeboat was patented on this day in 1845.

March 27

1. German scientist Wilhelm Konrad Roentgen, discoverer of the X-ray, was born on March 27, 1845.
2. The first coast-to-coast color TV broadcast took place on March 27, 1955.
3. Augusta Savage died on this date in 1962. He was a great sculptor.

March 28

1. Gunpowder was first used in Europe on March 28, 1380.
2. On this date in 1979, a nuclear accident took place at the Three Mile Island power plant near Harrisburg, Pennsylvania.
3. Czech educator Jan Amos Komensky, born today in 1592, wrote the first textbook in which the illustrations were as important as the text.
4. On March 28, 1797, the washing machine was patented by Nathaniel Briggs of New Hampshire.

March 29

1. Alice Parker became the first African-American woman to receive a United States patent. She did this on March 29, 1919, after designing a heating furnace that operated on gas instead of coal.
2. Our tenth president, John Tyler, was born on this date in 1790.
3. Hyman Lipman patented the first pencil with an eraser on this date in 1853.
4. Today is Vietnam Veteran's Day. The last U.S. troops left Vietnam on this day in 1973.

March 30

1. The United States acquired Alaska from Russia on this date in 1867.
2. The Fifteenth Amendment, providing for voting rights, was ratified on March 30, 1870.

Answer Key *(cont.)*

3. Vincent Van Gogh was born on March 30, 1853. Although he was Dutch, he painted most of his works in the countryside of France.

March 31

1. Air Force Captain Edward Dwight, Jr., became the first African American to be selected for training as an astronaut. He was selected on March 31, 1963.
2. Commodore Matthew C. Perry arranged the Open Door Treaty with Japan on March 31, 1854.
3. The first national advertisement for an automobile appeared on March 31, 1900, in the *Saturday Evening Post*. It featured the slogan "Automobiles that give satisfaction."
4. The Eiffel Tower, built by Alexandre Gustave Eiffel, was completed on March 31, 1889.

April 1

1. Beware! Today is April Fool's Day. This practice is thought to have originated in France before the use of the Gregorian calendar.
2. Charles R. Drew, a research physician, was born on April 1, 1904.
3. William Harvey, an English physician, was born on April 1, 1578. He was the first to discover the function of the heart in the circulation of blood through the body.
4. The United States orbited the first weather satellite on April 1, 1960.

April 2

1. The U.S. Mint was established in Philadelphia, Pennsylvania, on this date in 1792. George Washington provided his own household silver for the coins.
2. Hans Christian Andersen, a writer for young children, was born on April 2, 1805.
3. Howard University was established on April 2, 1867. It is located in Washington, D.C.

April 3

1. Ride 'em pony! The Pony Express began on April 3, 1860.
2. Washington Irving, a humorist and writer, was born on April 3, 1783.
3. Carter G. Woodson, an author and historian, was born today in 1875.

April 4

1. Our ninth president, William Henry Harrison, died on this date in 1841, only 32 days after his inauguration. He was the first president to die while in office.
2. On April 4, 1818, Congress decreed that the flag should have thirteen stripes and a star for each state.
3. Reverend Martin Luther King, Jr., was assassinated in Memphis, Tennessee, on April 4, 1968.
4. Maya Angelou, born on April 4, 1928, wrote the book *I Know Why the Caged Bird Sings*.

April 5

1. Booker Taliaferro Washington was born a slave on a Virginia plantation on April 5, 1856. He organized and served as the first president of Tuskegee Institute in Alabama.
2. Joseph Lister, founder of modern antiseptic surgery, was born on this date in 1827.
3. General Colin L. Powell was born on April 5, 1937.

April 6

1. Due to William Henry Harrison's death, John Tyler's presidential term began on April 6, 1841. Tyler became the first vice president to be sworn in under these circumstances.
2. Woodrow Wilson, our twenty-eighth president, declared war on Germany on this date in 1917. Germany had sunk several United States ships. The U.S. was now involved in World War I.
3. Admiral Robert E. Peary, Matthew Henson, and four Eskimos reached the North Pole on April 6, 1909.
4. The first modern Olympic Games were held in Athens, Greece, on April 6, 1896.

April 7

1. Lorraine Hansberry became the first African American to receive the New York Drama Critics' Circle Award. She won it on April 7, 1959, for her first play, *A Raisin in the Sun*.
2. Today is World Health Day.
3. Blues singer Billie Holiday was born on April 7, 1915. She was known as Lady Day.

April 8

1. Ponce de Leon, a Spanish explorer, landed in Florida on April 8, 1513.

Answer Key *(cont.)*

2. Many people were out of work in 1935. On this day, an emergency relief appropriation act was approved to provide employment to people who could carry out useful projects. It was called the Works Progress Administration.

3. James Tyng, a catcher on the Harvard baseball team, wore the first face protector on April 12, 1877.

April 9

1. The Civil War ended on April 9, 1865, when General Lee surrendered to General Grant.

2. On April 9, 1866, the first Civil Rights Act was passed, despite the veto of President Andrew Johnson. It was designed to protect the newly freed African Americans from repressive legislation. It set the stage for the passage of the Fourteenth Amendment.

3. The first free public library in the United States was established on April 9, 1833.

April 10

1. The U.S. patent system was established on April 10, 1790.

2. Today is Humane Day. The American Society for the Prevention of Cruelty to Animals was chartered on this date in 1866.

3. The first Arbor Day was April 10, 1872, in Nebraska. Arbor Day is celebrated at different times in different states.

April 11

1. Spelman College was organized on April 11, 1883.

2. Lyndon Johnson signed a Civil Rights Act on this date in 1968.

3. On April 11, 1947, Jackie Robinson became the first African American to play major league baseball. He played first base for the Brooklyn Dodgers.

April 12

1. Harry S Truman became president on April 12, 1945, following the death of President Roosevelt. Truman was our thirty-third president.

2. The Civil War began at Fort Sumter on this date in 1861.

3. On April 12, 1961, Soviet cosmonaut Yuri Gagarin became the first human to orbit Earth.

4. On this day in 1955, Dr. Jonas Salk announced the polio vaccine he had been testing was a success.

April 13

1. Thomas Jefferson, our third president, was born on this date in 1743.

2. Frank W. Woolworth, a merchant, was born on April 13, 1852.

3. Sidney Poitier was the first African American to win an Oscar for best performance by an actor. He won this award on April 13, 1964, for his role in *Lilies of the Field*.

4. The first elephant came to America on April 13, 1796. It came to New York City from Bengal, India.

April 14

1. John Wilkes Booth shot President Lincoln on this date in 1865.

2. The S.S. *Titanic* sank on April 14, 1912. This "unsinkable" boat sank after hitting an iceberg in the North Atlantic. It cost 1,517 passengers their lives.

3. Pocahontas married John Rolfe on April 14, 1614.

4. On April 14, 1828, Noah Webster completed the *American Dictionary of the English Language* after more than twenty years of work.

April 15

1. Andrew Johnson became our seventeenth president on April 15, 1865, following the death of President Lincoln.

2. The Revolutionary War ended on April 15, 1783.

3. Today is Income Tax Day. All state and federal income tax returns must be mailed.

4. Leonardo da Vinci was born on April 15, 1452. He painted the *Mona Lisa* and *The Last Supper*.

April 16

1. Wilbur Wright, an aviation pioneer, was born on April 16, 1867.

2. Major General Benjamin O. Davis, Jr., became the first African-American lieutenant general in the U.S. Air Force on April 16, 1960.

3. Basketball superstar Kareem Abdul-Jabbar was born on April 16, 1947.

Answer Key (cont.)

April 17
1. On April 17, 1542, Giovanni Verrazano discovered New York Harbor.
2. The first Ford Mustang was introduced on April 17, 1964.
3. *Surveyor III*, a lunar probe vehicle, landed on the moon on April 17, 1967. Its digging apparatus told NASA what the moon's surface was like.
4. On April 17, 1961, the United States launched the Bay of Pigs invasion in Cuba.

April 18
1. Paul Revere's ride took place on this date in 1775.
2. On April 18, 1906, San Francisco experienced a great earthquake and fire. It destroyed 10,000 acres of land and killed nearly 4,000 people.
3. The first store equipped with public washing machines in which people could do their laundry opened on April 18, 1934, in Forth Worth, Texas.

April 19
1. Today is Patriots' Day. The Battle of Lexington, the first major battle of the American Revolution, took place on April 19, 1775.
2. The Oklahoma City bombing, an act of terrorism, took place on April 19, 1995. It caused 168 deaths and injured 500 people.
3. The first U.S. automobile was built on this day in 1892.

April 20
1. Daniel Chester French, born on April 20, 1850, created the statue of Abraham Lincoln for the Lincoln Memorial in Washington, D.C.
2. On April 20, 1812, George Clinton became the first vice president of the United States to die in office.
3. On April 20, 1898, Pierre and Marie Curie uncovered the elements radium and polonium.

April 21
1. The Spanish-American War began on April 21, 1898.
2. It's Kindergarten Day! Friedrich Froebel, founder of the first kindergarten, was born on this date in 1782.
3. John Muir, a naturalist, was born today in 1838.

April 22
1. The first Earth Day was celebrated on April 22, 1970, focusing attention on environmental problems. Are you doing your part in conserving and recycling?
2. Oklahoma opened to settlers on April 22, 1889.
3. The first pair of roller skates was patented on April 22, 1823.

April 23
1. William Shakespeare was born on April 23, 1564, and died on April 23, 1616. He wrote *Romeo and Juliet*.
2. President James Buchanan, our fifteenth president, was born on this date in 1791.
3. The first public showing of a motion picture took place in New York City on April 23, 1896.
4. On April 23, 1985, Coca-Cola introduced New Coke. This variation on the popular soft drink did not sell well.

April 24
1. The Library of Congress was founded on April 24, 1800.
2. Robert Penn Warren, born on April 24, 1905, was named Poet Laureate by the Library of Congress in 1986.
3. The first American newspaper, the *Boston News-Letter*, was published by John Campbell on April 24, 1704.

April 25
1. Guglielmo Marconi, inventor of wireless telegraphy, was born on April 25, 1874.
2. A dog named Buddy became the first seeing-eye dog on this day in 1928.
3. Martin Waldseemuller was a geographer and mapmaker. On April 25, 1507, he published a geography book. On a map of the world he called a newly discovered continent "America."

April 26
1. John J. Audubon, an ornithologist, was born on April 26, 1785.
2. The nuclear accident at Chernobyl, USSR, took place on this date in 1986.
3. Today is the birthday of Charles Richter. In 1935, he developed a scale which measures the magnitude of earthquakes.

Answer Key *(cont.)*

April 27
1. Ulysses Simpson Grant was born on this date in 1822. Besides being our eighteenth president, he was commander of the Union troops during the Civil War.
2. Samuel Morse, inventor of the Morse code, was born on April 27, 1791.
3. Sierra Leone was proclaimed an independent nation on this date in 1961.
4. Ludwig Bemelmans was born on April 27, 1898. He is the writer of *Madeline*.

April 28
1. Maryland became the seventh state on April 28, 1788.
2. President James Monroe, our fifth president, was born on this date in 1758.
3. On April 28, 1919, Leslie Ervin made the first successful parachute jump.

April 29
1. On April 29, 1954, baseball great Willie Mays was voted the Most Valuable Player of the National League.
2. Swedish inventor Gideon Sundback patented the zipper on this date in 1913.
3. William Randolph Hearst, a newspaper publisher, was born on April 29, 1863.

April 30
1. Louisiana became the eighteenth state on April 30, 1812. It seceded on January 26, 1861, and was readmitted in July of 1868.
2. President George Washington was inaugurated on this date in 1789. The inauguration took place at Federal Hall in New York City, which was then our nation's capital.
3. Napoleon, the ruler of France, concluded the largest real estate transaction in world history on April 30, 1803. He sold the Louisiana Territory to President Jefferson.
4. Adolf Hitler died on this day in 1945.

May 1
1. The Empire State Building was completed on this day in 1930. This New York monument is 102 stories high.
2. Orson Welles' film *Citizen Kane* premiered on May 1, 1941. Many film critics consider it the finest film ever made.
3. On May 1, 1963, James Whitaker became the first American to climb Mount Everest.

May 2
1. The Hudson Bay Company was chartered on May 2, 1670.
2. Elijah McCoy, born in Canada on May 2, 1844, invented the lubricator cup. His invention dripped oil continuously to oil machinery parts so they did not have to be shut down.
3. On May 2, 1932, Pearl S. Buck was awarded the Pulitzer Prize for fiction for her book *The Good Earth*.

May 3
1. The first United States school of medicine was established in Philadelphia on May 3, 1765.
2. The World's Columbian Exposition opened in Chicago on May 3, 1893. Often called "The White City," the exposition used more electricity than the whole city of Chicago at that time.
3. Golda Meir was born on May 3, 1898. Her family and she emigrated from Kiev, Russia, to Milwaukee, Wisconsin. She eventually became prime minister of Israel.
4. The first comic book was published on this day in 1934.

May 4
1. Horace Mann, an educator, was born on May 4, 1796.
2. Today is National Weather Observer's Day!
3. Peter Minuit landed on Manhattan on May 4, 1626. He eventually purchased the island from the Native Americans living there.
4. Actress Audrey Hepburn was born on May 4, 1929.

May 5
1. On May 5, 1862, a group of poorly armed Mexican soldiers defeated thousands of well-armed professional French soldiers at Puebla, Mexico. Cinco de Mayo, which commemorates this victory, is celebrated by people of Mexican descent.
2. The first suborbital space flight was made by Alan B. Shepard on May 5, 1961.
3. Nellie Bly, born on May 5, 1867, used the pen name Elizabeth Cochran. She was the first American woman journalist to achieve international fame.
4. On this day in 1961, the federal minimum

Answer Key *(cont.)*

wage was raised to $1.25 an hour. Do you know what the current federal minimum wage is?

May 6
1. President Dwight D. Eisenhower signed the Civil Rights Act of 1960 on May 6th.
2. Robert E. Peary, an Arctic explorer, was born on May 6, 1856.
3. The first postage stamp was issued in England on this date in 1840.
4. This is the halfway point of spring. There are as many days until summer begins as have passed since the last day of winter.
5. Hall of Fame baseball player Willie Mays was born on May 6, 1931.

May 7
1. The liner *Lusitania* was sunk in the Atlantic Ocean by a German submarine on May 7, 1915.
2. Robert Browning was born on May 7, 1812. He wrote "The Pied Piper of Hamelin."
3. Peter Ilich Tchaikovsky, a famous Russian composer, was born on May 7, 1840. Sixteen years earlier, on the very same day, Beethoven's Ninth Symphony debuted.
4. On May 7, 1959, 93,103 spectators gathered at the Los Angeles Coliseum to honor catcher Roy Campanella, who had been paralyzed in a traffic accident a year earlier. It was the largest crowd ever assembled to witness a baseball game.

May 8
1. Today is V-E Day. Germany surrendered on May 8, 1945, ending World War II. The war began September 1, 1939, when Germany attacked Poland.
2. President Harry S Truman was born on May 8, 1884.
3. Jean H. Dunant, a Swiss, was born today in 1828. He founded the International Red Cross.
4. The French celebrate Joan of Arc Day each May 8th.

May 9
1. The first comic strip was published on May 9, 1754, by Benjamin Franklin.
2. James Pollard Espy, a meteorologist who started scientific weather prediction, was born on this date in 1785.

3. John Brown, an abolitionist, was born on May 9, 1800.
4. James M. Barrie, born May 9, 1860, was an English author. His play *Peter Pan* is set in Never-Never Land, a place where no one grows up.

May 10
1. It's Golden Spike Day! The completion of the first transcontinental railroad happened on May 10, 1869.
2. There was excitement on May 10, 1927, when the Hotel Statler in Boston, Massachusetts, offered two radio channels to guests. Thirteen hundred rooms were equipped with headsets, but only one person could listen at a time.
3. On this day in 1872, Victoria Woodhull became the first female to run for the office of president of the United States of America.

May 11
1. Minnesota became the thirty-second state on May 11, 1858.
2. Ottmar Merganthaler, inventor of the Linotype, was born on May 11, 1854.
3. Today is the birth date of William Grant Still. He was a composer of musicals, symphonies, and operas. He was born in 1895.
4. Today in 1947, the B. F. Goodrich Company started to manufacture tubeless tires.

May 12
1. Florence Nightingale, the English founder of modern nursing, was born on May 12, 1820.
2. May 12, 1812, is the birth date of Edward Lear. His name is synonymous with limericks.
3. Baseball legend Yogi Berra was born on May 12, 1925. He's known for saying such things as "It ain't over 'til it's over."

May 13
1. Heavyweight boxing champion Joe Louis was born on May 13, 1914, in Chambers County, Alabama.
2. The United States declared war on Mexico on May 13, 1846.
3. Jamestown, Virginia, the first permanent English settlement in North America, was founded on May 13, 1607.

Answer Key *(cont.)*

4. Singer Stevie Wonder was born on May 13, 1951.

May 14

1. Gabriel D. Fahrenheit was born on May 14, 1686. His system marks 32 degrees as the freezing point and 212 degrees as boiling.
2. Lewis and Clark began exploring Louisiana and the Northwest Territories on this day in 1804.
3. It's midnight sun at North Cape. From May 14 until July 30, the sun never goes below the horizon at this island.
4. On May 14, 1908, Charles W. Furnas became the first passenger to fly in an airplane. He flew with Wilbur Wright.

May 15

1. The first air mail service flight took place on May 15, 1918.
2. Gertrude Elise Ayer was the first female African-American public school principal in New York. She became principal on May 15, 1935.
3. Ellen Church, a trained nurse, became the first airplane stewardess on this date in 1930.
4. On this date in 1940, the first successful helicopter flight in the U.S. took place.
5. L. Frank Baum, author of *The Wonderful Wizard of Oz* (1900) was born on May 15, 1856.

May 16

1. Elizabeth Peabody was born on May 16, 1804. She is the founder of the first United States kindergarten.
2. On May 16, 1866, Congress authorized the creation of the nickel.
3. The first Academy Awards ceremony was held on this day in 1929.

May 17

1. Father Jacques Marquette and Louis Joliet began exploring the Mississippi River on May 17, 1673.
2. Happy Birthday, New York Stock Exchange! On May 17, 1792, about two dozen merchants and brokers agreed to form a group for buying and selling stocks.
3. The landmark Supreme Court decision in the case of *Brown vs. Board of Education of Topeka, Kansas*, was declared on May 17, 1954. This ruling stated that racial segregation in public schools was unconstitutional.

May 18

1. Mount St. Helens erupted on May 18, 1980, causing loss of life, fires, mud slides, and floods.
2. The Canadian city of Montreal was founded on this day in 1642.
3. On May 18, 1852, Massachusetts became the first state to pass a law which made school attendance mandatory for school-age children.

May 19

1. The Ringling Brothers Circus opened in Baraboo, Wisconsin, on May 19, 1884.
2. Malcolm X was born Malcolm Little on May 19, 1925. He became famous as a leader of the black religious movement named the Nation of Islam.
3. Mary McLeod Bethrune, a dedicated educator and civic leader, died on May 19, 1955, in Daytona Beach, Florida.
4. Today is dark day in New England. At midday in 1780, the sky in New England suddenly became dark. No one is sure why this happened.

May 20

1. The Homestead Act was signed on May 20, 1862.
2. Dolley Payne Madison, wife of the fourth president, was born on May 20, 1768. She's famous for saving the portrait of George Washington when the British burned the capital in 1812.
3. Amelia Earhart began the first solo flight ever by a woman on May 20, 1932.

May 21

1. The American Red Cross was organized on May 21, 1881. Clara Barton, a Civil War nurse, was its founder.
2. The first bicycles were imported into the United States on May 21, 1891.
3. Charles A. Lindbergh completed his first solo transatlantic flight on this date in 1927.
4. Glenn H. Curtiss, born on May 21, 1878, helped design the first plane sold commercially. It was called the June Bug. In 1909 it sold for $5,000.

Answer Key *(cont.)*

May 22
1. The *Savannah*, the first American ship, made the transatlantic crossing under steam power. It started from Savannah, Georgia, on May 22, 1819. The trip to Liverpool, England, took 29 days.
2. Benjamin O. Davis, Jr., of the United States Air Force became the first African American in U.S. military history to be promoted to the rank of major general. This happened on May 22, 1959.
3. Sir Arthur Conan Doyle was born on May 22, 1859. He created the famous detective Sherlock Holmes.

May 23
1. South Carolina was the eighth state to ratify the Constitution. It did so on May 23, 1788. It then seceded on December 20, 1860, and was readmitted in 1868.
2. Carolus Linnaeus was born on this day in 1707. He is known as the "father of biology."
3. On May 23, 1975, Junko Tabei, a Japanese housewife, became the first woman to reach the top of Mt. Everest.

May 24
1. Samuel F. B. Morse sent the first telegraph message on May 24, 1844.
2. Today marks the death of Edward Kennedy "Duke" Ellington. He died on this date in 1974.
3. On May 24, 1983, hundreds of people walked across the Brooklyn Bridge in New York City. They were celebrating the 100th anniversary of the opening of this bridge to traffic.

May 25
1. Ralph Waldo Emerson, a philosopher and writer, was born on May 25, 1803.
2. The film *Star Wars* premiered on May 25, 1977.
3. On May 25, 1986, 7,000,000 people participated in Hands Across America. The purpose of the demonstration was to bring attention to the problem of homelessness in America.

May 26
1. Paine College was founded in Augusta, Georgia, on May 26, 1864.
2. The last Confederate troops in the Civil War surrendered in Shreveport, Louisiana, on May 26, 1865.
3. Actor John Wayne was born today in 1907.
4. Sally Kirsten Ride was born in Encino, California, on May 26, 1951. On January 16, 1978, she became the first woman candidate to become an astronaut.

May 27
1. The Golden Gate Bridge opened in San Francisco on May 27, 1937.
2. Julia Ward Howe, author of the "Battle Hymn of the Republic," was born on this date in 1819.
3. Isadora Duncan, a dancer, was born on May 27, 1878.

May 28
1. Booker T. Washington became the first African American to be elected to the Hall of Fame of Great Americans. It happened on May 28, 1945.
2. John Muir formed the Sierra Club on May 28, 1892.
3. Jim Thorpe, born on May 28, 1886, was one of the world's most versatile athletes. He played professional football, won fame as a track-and-field champion, and played major-league baseball.

May 29
1. President John Fitzgerald Kennedy was born on May 29, 1917, in Brookline, Massachusetts, a suburb of Boston. Jack, as his family called him, was our thirty-fifth president.
2. Rhode Island became the thirteenth state of the Union on May 29, 1790.
3. Wisconsin became the thirtieth state on May 29, 1848.
4. Patrick Henry, an American Revolution leader and orator, was born on May 29, 1736.

May 30
1. No one knows exactly when Memorial Day was first observed. According to tradition, Memorial Day originated during the Civil War when some Southern women chose May 30th to decorate soldiers' graves.
2. Christopher Columbus began his third voyage on May 30, 1498.

Answer Key *(cont.)*

3. The Lincoln Memorial was dedicated on May 30, 1922. It's located in Washington, D.C.
4. The compact disc was first introduced on this day in 1981.

May 31
1. On May 31, 1819, Walt Whitman, an American poet, was born. He wrote *Leaves of Grass*.
2. Today is Indianapolis 500 race day.
3. The United States copyright law was enacted on May 31, 1790.
4. On May 31, 1933, a patent was given to Gerald Brown for making "invisible" glass. The patent was for a process that would reduce the amount of reflection on glass windows.

June 1
1. Kentucky achieved statehood on June 1, 1792. It was the second to do so after the original thirteen colonies.
2. Tennessee became the sixteenth state on June 1, 1796. It seceded on June 24, 1861, and was readmitted on July 24, 1866.
3. Jacques Marquette, a French explorer, was born on June 1, 1637.
4. Brigham Young, leader of the Mormons, was born on this date in 1801.

June 2
1. On June 2, 1875, Alexander Graham Bell heard a sound on his invention, the telephone.
2. A swimming pool built in the White House was formally accepted and opened by President Franklin Roosevelt on July 2, 1933.
3. On this day in 1941, baseball great Lou Gehrig died at age 37 of a disease which now bears his name. At his retirement ceremony, Gehrig said "Today I consider myself the luckiest man on the face of the earth."

June 3
1. Jefferson Davis, president of the Confederate States of America, was born on June 3, 1808.
2. Dr. Charles Drew was born on this date in 1904. He was a blood plasma researcher.
3. The ballad "Casey at the Bat" was first printed in the *San Francisco Examiner* on June 3, 1888.

4. The New York Knickerbockers, a baseball team, introduced the first baseball uniforms on June 3, 1851.

June 4
1. On June 4, 1896, Henry Ford introduced his first car, the Quadra Cycle.
2. The first Baptist church in America was founded on June 4, 1665.
3. On June 4, 1781, Jack Jouett rode 45 miles and 6 $\frac{1}{2}$ hours to warn Virginia's Governor Thomas Jefferson and the legislature that the British were coming.
4. On June 4, 1965, Major Ed White became the first American to walk in space.

June 5
1. Senator Robert F. Kennedy was shot by an assassin on June 5, 1968.
2. On June 5, 1956, the Federal courts ruled that segregation on the Montgomery city buses was unconstitutional.
3. The first hot-air balloon flight, by the Montgolfier brothers, took place in France on June 5, 1783.
4. Today is World Environment Day! Activities are held to show concern for the preservation and enhancement of the environment.

June 6
1. Today is D-Day. On June 6, 1944, the British, Canadians, and Americans invaded the beaches of Normandy.
2. On June 6, 1932, the U.S. government passed a law that placed a tax of one cent a gallon on gasoline and other motor fuel.
3. On this day in 1872, Susan B. Anthony was fined for trying to vote. At that time women were not allowed to vote.

June 7
1. Gwendolyn Brooks was born on June 7, 1917. She is a well-known black poet.
2. A horse named Gallant Fox won the Belmont Stakes on this day in 1930. With this victory, Gallant Fox became only the second horse to win the Triple Crown of horse racing.
3. To capture the Triple Crown of horse racing, a horse has to win the Preakness Stakes, the Kentucky Derby, and the Belmont Stakes in the same year.

Answer Key *(cont.)*

June 8
1. Frank Lloyd Wright, an architect, was born on June 8, 1869.
2. On June 8, 1953, the Supreme Court banned discrimination in restaurants in Washington, D.C.
3. Barbara Bush, wife of President George Bush, was born today in 1925.
4. Ice cream was first advertised and sold in America on June 8, 1786.

June 9
1. Meta Vaux Warwick Fuller, the foremost African-American sculptress in the 19th century, was born on June 9, 1877.
2. Cole Porter, a composer, was born on June 9, 1893.
3. Donald Duck appeared in a short cartoon on June 9, 1934.

June 10
1. Jack Johnson, the first African-American heavyweight boxing champion, died on June 10, 1946.
2. Maurice Sendak was born today in 1928. He is the illustrator and author of many books, including *Where the Wild Things Are*.
3. The first drive-through restaurant opened on this day in 1952.

June 11
1. French oceanographer Jacques Cousteau was born on June 11, 1910.
2. Jeannette Rankin was born near Missoula, Montana, on June 11, 1880. She was the first woman to be elected to the U.S. House of Representatives.
3. Quarterback Joe Montana was born on June 11, 1956. He led the San Francisco 49ers to four Super Bowl victories.

June 12
1. Medgar Evers was assassinated on June 12, 1963. At the time, he was head of the Mississippi NAACP.
2. Today is the celebration of the invention of baseball. It was named for the four bases the batter must touch to score a run.
3. George Bush, our forty-first president, was born on June 12, 1924.
4. On June 12, 1967, a Soviet space capsule landed on the surface of the planet Venus.

June 13
1. The Department of Labor was created on June 13, 1888.
2. Football hero "Red" Grange was born on June 13, 1903. He was nicknamed "the Galloping Ghost."
3. On June 13, 1966, the U.S. Supreme Court ruled that when someone is arrested, he or she doesn't have to say anything until a lawyer is present. These are called the Miranda rights.

June 14
1. Today is Flag Day! Flags have been used since ancient times as symbols.
2. Harriet Beecher Stowe, author of *Uncle Tom's Cabin*, was born on June 14, 1811.
3. Congress established the United States Army on June 14, 1775.

June 15
1. Arkansas became the twenty-fifth state on June 15, 1836. It seceded on May 6, 1861, and was readmitted on June 22, 1868.
2. Ben Franklin's historic kite-flying experiment, proving lightning was composed of electricity, took place on June 15, 1752.
3. The Magna Carta was granted by King John on June 15, 1215.
4. The first nonstop transatlantic flight arrived in Ireland on June 15, 1919.
5. Henry O. Flipper became the first African-American graduate of West Point on June 15, 1877.

June 16
1. The Ford Motor Company was founded on June 16, 1903.
2. James Joyce's famous novel *Ulysses* tells the story of one day in the life of three different people. That day is June 16, 1904.
3. The first woman in space, Valentina Tereshkova, spoke these words on June 16, 1963: "It is I, Sea Gull...." She was a twenty-six-year-old Soviet cosmonaut at the time.

June 17
1. The Battle of Bunker Hill began on June 17, 1775.

Answer Key *(cont.)*

2. Explorers Father Jacques Marquette and Louis Joliet discovered the Mississippi River on June 17, 1673.
3. On June 17, 1972, five burglars were arrested for being in the offices of the Democratic National Committee in the Watergate building in Washington, D.C.
4. Barry Manilow was born on June 17, 1946. He's known as a singer, composer, and arranger.

June 18
1. Napoleon was defeated at Waterloo on June 18, 1815.
2. On June 18, 1988, fourteen students at Hanover High School, New Hampshire, made the *Guiness Book of World Records* by playing leapfrog. They played for eight days. That's 189 hours and 49 minutes at a distance of 888.1 miles.
3. Sally Kirsten Ride became the first American woman in space on June 18, 1983.
4. Comic strip character Garfield appeared for the first time on June 18, 1978.

June 19
1. On June 19, 1885, the Statue of Liberty arrived in the New York harbor from France.
2. The first recorded baseball game was played at Elysian Fields in Hoboken, New Jersey, on June 19, 1846.
3. Father's Day was first celebrated in Spokane, Washington, on June 19, 1910.

June 20
1. West Virginia became the thirty-fifth state on June 20, 1863.
2. Congress adopted the design for the Great Seal of the U.S. on June 20, 1782.
3. Eli Whitney applied for the patent of the cotton gin on June 20, 1793.
4. To celebrate the coming summer season, Fairbanks, Alaska, has a midnight sun baseball game that begins about 10:30 P.M. and is played without artificial lights.

June 21
1. New Hampshire was the ninth state to ratify the United States Constitution. It did so on June 21, 1787.
2. Daniel Carter Beard was born on June 21, 1850. He was a naturalist, writer,

illustrator, and founder of the Boy Scouts in the U.S.
3. Today is the traditional date for the beginning of summer.

June 22
1. The Department of Justice was founded on June 22, 1870.
2. On June 22, 1970, the U.S. adopted the Twenty-sixth Amendment, which lowered the voting age from 21 to 18.
3. On June 22, 1943, W.E.B. Du Bois became the first African American to be elected to membership in the National Institute of Arts and Letters.
4. Journalist Ed Bradley from *60 Minutes* was born today in 1941.

June 23
1. William Penn signed a treaty with the Indians on June 23, 1683.
2. Irving S. Cobb, born June 23, 1876, was a humorous writer of short stories and novels. He believed that "you had to poke fun at yourself before you could poke fun at anyone else without hurting his feelings."
3. Olympic track star Wilma Rudolph was born on June 23, 1940.

June 24
1. John Cabot discovered North America's mainland on June 24, 1497.
2. Henry Ward Beecher, a clergyman and orator, was born on this date in 1813.
3. Gustavus Franklin Swift was born on this date in 1839. He was 17 when he went into the butchering business. In 1875 Swift went to Chicago and opened the first slaughterhouse.
4. John Ciardi, one of America's foremost contemporary poets, was born on June 24, 1916.

June 25
1. General George Custer's forces were destroyed by Sioux and Cheyenne Indians at Little Big Horn on June 25, 1876, in Montana. The Indians were led by Sitting Bull.
2. Virginia was the tenth state to ratify the Constitution. It did so on June 25, 1788. It seceded on April 17, 1861, and was readmitted on January 26, 1870.
3. The Korean War began on June 25, 1950.
4. On June 25, 1941, President Roosevelt

Answer Key *(cont.)*

created the Committee on Fair Employment Practices.

June 26
1. The United Nations charter was signed on June 26, 1945.
2. Novelist Pearl S. Buck was born on this date in 1892.
3. On June 26, 1959, the St. Lawrence Seaway was dedicated and officially opened.
4. Babe Didrikson Zaharias, one of the greatest female athletes of all time, was born on June 26, 1911. Babe excelled at several sports.

June 27
1. Today is the birth date of Helen Keller. She was born on this date in 1880.
2. Poet Paul Laurence Dunbar was born on June 27, 1872.
3. James Smithson, who died today in 1829, left his great wealth to start a museum in Washington, D.C. That museum is called the Smithsonian Institution.

June 28
1. Archduke Francis Ferdinand of Austria was assassinated on June 28, 1914. This was the start of World War I.
2. The Versailles Treaty was signed on June 28, 1918. World War I was officially over.
3. John Elway, longtime quarterback of the Denver Broncos, was born on June 28, 1960. Elway holds the record for most victories by a quarterback in professional football history.

June 29
1. George W. Goethals, the engineer who supervised the building of the Panama Canal, was born on June 29, 1858.
2. William James Mayo was born on this date in 1861. He was the surgeon who helped establish the Mayo Foundation.
3. As a college freshman, Charles Dumas became the first person to make a high jump of seven feet, one-half inch. He did it on this date in 1956.
4. Born in Seigen, Germany, on June 29, 1577, Peter Paul Rubens became one of the greatest Flemish painters of the 1600s.

June 30
1. Zaire was proclaimed an independent nation on June 30, 1960.
2. The Pure Food and Drug Act was signed on this date in 1906.
3. On June 30, 1940, the U.S. Fish and Wildlife Service was established.
4. On June 30, 1908, a huge meteorite landed in central Siberia. People as far away as 466 miles saw it in full daylight; the blast was felt 50 miles away.
5. Bondin crossed Niagara Falls on a rope 1,100 feet long on June 30, 1859.

July 1
1. Somali was proclaimed an independent nation on July 1, 1960.
2. The first U.S. postage stamps were issued on this date in 1847.
3. The Battle of Gettysburg began on July 1, 1863.
4. Today is Dominion Day! The Dominion of Canada was established on July 1, 1863.

July 2
1. Lyndon Baines Johnson, our thirty-sixth president, signed the Civil Rights bill on July 2, 1964. Martin Luther King, Jr., was present for this momentous occasion.
2. Supreme Court Justice Thurgood Marshall was born on July 2, 1908.
3. The Continental Congress declared U.S. independence from England on July 2, 1776.
4. President James Garfield was assassinated on this date in 1881.

July 3
1. Idaho became the forty-third state on July 3, 1890.
2. John Singleton Copley, a painter, was born on July 3, 1738.
3. George M. Cohan, a composer, was born on this date in 1878.

July 4
1. Thomas Jefferson died on this date in 1826. Coincidentally, it's the anniversary of the Declaration of Independence, which was written in 1776.
2. Calvin Coolidge, our thirtieth president, was born on July 4, 1872. He was vice president to President Harding and took office following Harding's death on August 2, 1923.
3. Stephen Foster, a composer, was born on July 4, 1826.

Answer Key *(cont.)*

July 5
1. David G. Farragut was born on July 5, 1801. He was the first admiral of the U.S. Navy.
2. Phineas Taylor Barnum was born on July 5, 1810. He was a showman and circus promoter.
3. On July 5, 1975, Arthur Ashe became the first African American to win the men's tennis singles championship at Wimbledon.

July 6
1. Malawi was proclaimed an independent nation on July 6, 1964.
2. Naval hero John Paul Jones was born on July 6, 1747.
3. The Republican Party was named on July 6, 1854.
4. Beatrix Potter, creator of Peter Rabbit, was born on this date in 1866.
5. The first all-star baseball game took place on July 6, 1933. Legend has it that on that day, Babe Ruth pointed to the outfield fence before hitting a home run there on the very next pitch!

July 7
1. Hawaii was annexed by the United States on July 7, 1898.
2. Carlo Lorenzini, whose pen name was Carlo Collodi, published the first chapter of his classic tale *Pinocchio* on July 7, 1881.
3. Sandra Day O'Connor was the first woman justice of the United States Supreme Court. She was sworn in on July 7, 1981.

July 8
1. While tolling the death of Chief Justice John Marshall on July 8, 1835, the Liberty Bell cracked.
2. The *Wall Street Journal* was first published on July 8, 1889.
3. The first ice-cream sundae was served on this day in 1881.

July 9
1. Our twelfth president, Zachary Taylor, died on this date in 1850. He had only been in office for sixteen months when he suffered a sunstroke while taking part in the ceremonies at the then-unfinished Washington Monument on the Fourth of July.
2. John D. Rockefeller, Sr., an industrialist and philanthropist, was born on July 9, 1839.
3. Elias Howe was born on this date in 1819. He patented the sewing machine in 1846.

July 10
1. Millard Fillmore took the presidency after the death of Zachary Taylor. He was our thirteenth president. He modernized the White House by putting in the first bathtub with running water and adding a room for a library.
2. Wyoming became the forty-fourth state on July 10, 1890.
3. On July 10, 1790, Washington, D.C., was chosen as the site of our nation's capital.
4. Mary Bethune, an educator, was born on July 10, 1875.

July 11
1. President John Quincy Adams was born on July 11, 1767.
2. The U.S. Air Force Academy was established on July 11, 1955.
3. Elwyn Brooks White was born on July 11, 1899. He is best known as E. B. White, author of *Stuart Little* (1945), *Charlotte's Web* (1952), and *The Trumpet of the Swan* (1970).

July 12
1. George Eastman, a photography pioneer, was born on July 12, 1854.
2. The Medal of Honor was established on July 12, 1861.
3. Aaron Burr killed Alexander Hamilton in a duel on July 12, 1804.
4. Comedian Bill Cosby was born on July 12, 1938, and American writer Henry David Thoreau was born on July 12, 1817.

July 13
1. Congress passed the Northwest Ordinance on July 13, 1787.
2. Women began competing in the Olympics on July 13, 1908.
3. Erno Rubik, inventor of the Rubik's Cube, was born on July 13, 1944.

July 14
1. Gerald Rudolph Ford, our thirty-eighth president, was born on July 14, 1913. He was the first vice president not elected by the people to become president. This followed the resignation of President Nixon.

Answer Key *(cont.)*

2. Today is Bastille Day (Independence Day) in France. On July 14, 1789, the people of Paris captured the Bastille, an old fortress and prison.
3. Edwin James made his ascent of Pikes Peak on July 14, 1820.

July 15
1. Wiley Post began his first round-the-world solo flight on July 15, 1933.
2. Clement Moore, author of *A Visit from St. Nicholas*, was born on this date in 1779.
3. On this day in 1965, Congress passed a law which required all cigarette packages to display a health warning.

July 16
1. Alamogordo, New Mexico, was the desert area used as an experimental drop site for the first atomic bomb. The bomb was dropped on July 16, 1945. The mushroom cloud rose 41,000 feet into the air. It left a half-mile-wide crater with a glassy, radioactive crust.
2. Roald Amundsen, a Norwegian explorer and discoverer of the South Pole, was born on July 16, 1872.
3. Arnold Adoff was born on July 16, 1935. In November of 1988, Adoff received the eighth National Council of Teachers of English Award for Excellence in Poetry for Children.

July 17
1. John Jacob Astor, financier and fur merchant, was born on July 17, 1763.
2. Spain ceded Florida to the United States on July 17, 1819.
3. Disneyland was founded on this day in 1955.

July 18
1. Tennis was introduced in the United States on July 18, 1874.
2. The Presidential Succession Act was signed on July 18, 1947.
3. At the age of 14, Nadia Comaneci became the first gymnast to receive a perfect score in the Olympic Games. It happened on July 18, 1976.

July 19
1. The first women's right convention was held in Seneca Falls, New York, on July 19, 1848.

2. Samuel Colt, inventor of the repeating pistol, was born on this date in 1814.
3. Poet Eve Merriam was born on July 19, 1916.
4. Karla Kuskin, a native New Yorker and a writer of prose and poetry, was born on July 19, 1932.

July 20
1. On July 20, 1969, United States Astronaut Neil A. Armstrong, commander of the *Apollo 11*, became the first person to set foot on the moon. He said, "That's one small step for man, one giant leap for mankind."
2. The first draft number of World War I was drawn on July 20, 1917.
3. Georgia joined the colonies on July 20, 1770.

July 21
1. The first Battle of Bull Run took place on July 21, 1861.
2. The U.S. Veteran's Administration was established on July 21, 1930.
3. Actor and comedian Robin Williams was born today in 1952.

July 22
1. Moses Cleveland founded Cleveland, Ohio, on July 22, 1796.
2. Alexander MacKenzie was the first man to cross North America. He reached the Pacific Ocean on July 22, 1793.
3. Poet Carl Sandburg died on July 22, 1967.
4. Emma Lazarus wrote the poem for the Statue of Liberty. She was born on July 22, 1849.

July 23
1. The first typewriter was patented on July 23, 1829.
2. The Bunker Hill Monument was completed on this date in 1841.
3. General William Booth founded the Salvation Army in England on July 23, 1865.
4. The ice-cream cone was introduced at St. Louis World's Fair on July 23, 1904.

July 24
1. Amelia Earhart was born on July 24, 1897. She was an aviator, writer, and lecturer.
2. Salt Lake City, Utah, was founded on July 24, 1847, by a group of Mormons led by Brigham Young.

Answer Key *(cont.)*

3. On July 24, 1783, Simon Bolivar was born. He is known as the father of these five countries: Venezuela, Ecuador, Columbia, Peru, and Bolivia.

July 25

1. The continent of Antarctica was discovered on July 25, 1820.
2. Puerto Rico became a commonwealth on July 25, 1952.
3. On this day in 1983, the temperature in Antarctica dipped to 129 degrees below zero. That is the lowest natural temperature ever recorded.

July 26

1. New York became the eleventh state to ratify the Constitution. It did so on July 26, 1788.
2. The U.S. Postal Service began on July 26, 1775.
3. On July 26, 1965, Great Britain granted independence to the Maldive Islands, which lie four hundred miles southwest of Ceylon in the Indian Ocean.

July 27

1. The first successful transatlantic cable was completed on July 27, 1866.
2. The U.S. State Department was established on this date in 1789.
3. The Korean Armistice was signed on July 27, 1953.

July 28

1. World War I began on July 28, 1914.
2. The Fourteenth Amendment to the Constitution was effective on July 28, 1868.
3. Today is National Joseph Lee Day. We are honoring the founder of playgrounds.
4. *Skylab 2* was launched from Cape Kennedy, Florida, on July 28, 1973. The crew spent a record-breaking 59 days in space. Cape Kennedy is now called Cape Canaveral.

July 29

1. Booth Tarkington, a novelist, was born on July 29, 1869.
2. President Eisenhower signed the National Aeronautics and Space Act (NASA) on this day in 1958.
3. The International Atomic Energy Agency was established on July 29, 1957.

July 30

1. The first representative assembly in America took place in Jamestown, Virginia, on July 30, 1619.
2. Henry Ford, auto manufacturer and philanthropist, was born on July 30, 1863.
3. "In God We Trust" became an official U.S. motto on July 30, 1956.
4. Actor Arnold Schwarzenegger was born on July 30, 1947, in Austria.

July 31

1. The first U.S. patent was granted on July 31, 1790. It was granted to Samuel Hopkins of Vermont for a soap-making process using potash and pearl ash.
2. American President George Bush and Soviet President Mikhail Gorbachev signed the Strategic Arms Reduction Treaty on this day in 1991.
3. Construction began on the U.S. Mint in Washington, D.C., on this day in 1792.

August 1

1. Herman Melville, author of *Moby Dick*, was born on August 1, 1819.
2. Colorado became the thirty-eighth state on August 1, 1876.
3. The U.S. Army Air Force was established on August 1, 1907.
4. Francis Scott Key, author of "The Star-Spangled Banner," was born today in 1779.

August 2

1. Inventor Andrew Hallidie piloted San Francisco's first cable car down Nob Hill at 5:00 A.M. on August 2, 1873.
2. The U.S. bought the first military plane from the Wright Brothers on August 2, 1909.
3. James Baldwin, a novelist and essayist, was born in Harlem, New York, on August 2, 1924.

August 3

1. The country of Niger was proclaimed an independent nation on August 3, 1960.
2. Columbus sailed westward from Spain on August 3, 1492. The voyage was made aboard the *Niña*, *Pinta*, and *Santa Maria*.
3. The USS *Nautilus* became the first ship to reach the North Pole. It did so on August 3, 1958.

August 4

1. The U.S. Coast Guard was established on

Answer Key (cont.)

August 4, 1790.

2. President Jimmy Carter signed the Energy Organization Act on this day in 1977.
3. Federal income tax was first collected in the United States on August 4, 1862.

August 5

1. Upper Volta was proclaimed an independent nation on August 5, 1960.
2. Actress Marilyn Monroe died on this day in 1962.
3. Neil Armstrong was born on August 5, 1930. What accomplishment was he the first person to achieve?

August 6

1. The atomic bomb was dropped on Hiroshima, Japan, on August 6, 1945.
2. On August 6, 1926, Gertrude Ederle became the first woman to swim the English Channel.
3. President Lyndon B. Johnson signed the Voting Rights Act on this day in 1965.

August 7

1. The International Peace Bridge was dedicated on August 7, 1927. This commemorated the long-lasting peace between the U.S. and Canada.
2. George Stephenson invented the steam locomotive on August 7, 1815.
3. Ralph Bunche, statesman, social scientist, diplomat, United Nations representative, and winner of the Nobel Peace Prize, was born on August 7, 1904, in Detroit, Michigan.

August 8

1. The Ivory Coast was proclaimed an independent nation on August 8, 1960.
2. Marjorie Kinnan Rawlings, a novelist, was born on August 8, 1896.
3. Today is Intertribal Indian Ceremonial Day. The ceremony takes place in Gallup, New Mexico.
4. An artificial heart pump was successfully implanted for the first time on August 8, 1966.

August 9

1. Our thirty-seventh president, Richard Milhous Nixon, was the first president ever to resign from office. He resigned on August 9, 1974, due to the Watergate scandal.
2. English writer Izaak Walton, known as the "father of angling," was born on August 9, 1593.
3. On August 9, 1945, the U.S. dropped an atomic bomb on Nagasaki, Japan.
4. Baseball/football player Deion Sanders was born on August 9, 1967.

August 10

1. Missouri became the twenty-fourth state on August 10, 1821.
2. President Herbert C. Hoover, our thirty-first president, was born on August 10, 1874.
3. The Smithsonian Institution was established in Washington, D.C., on August 10, 1846.

August 11

1. Chad was proclaimed an independent nation on August 11, 1960.
2. The nation of Chad is located on the continent of Africa.
3. Alex Haley, author of the Pulitzer Prize-winning novel *Roots*, was born on August 11, 1921.

August 12

1. The first police force was established in America on August 12, 1658.
2. Thomas Edison invented the phonograph on this day in 1877.
3. Isaac Singer patented his sewing machine on this day in 1851.

August 13

1. Manila surrendered to U.S. forces on August 13, 1898.
2. Lucy Stone, a women's rights leader, was born on August 13, 1818.
3. Sharpshooter Annie Oakley was born on this date in 1860.

August 14

1. The Social Security Act was approved on August 14, 1935.
2. Julia Child, a famous chef, was born on August 14, 1912.
3. The Atlantic Charter was issued on this date in 1941 by American President Franklin D. Roosevelt and British Prime Minister Winston Churchill.

August 15

1. Japan surrendered on August 15, 1945, after the atomic bomb was dropped on the city of Hiroshima and then Nagasaki.

Answer Key (cont.)

World War II had ended.

2. Congo Brazzaville was proclaimed an independent nation on August 15, 1960.
3. The Panama Canal was opened on this date in 1914.
4. Napoleon Bonaparte was born on August 15, 1769.
5. The famous Woodstock music festival began on this day in 1969. It lasted three days.

August 16

1. The Battle of Bennington, Virginia, took place on August 16, 1777.
2. Elvis Presley died on this day in 1977. His home in Memphis, Tennessee, is called Graceland.
3. Pop singer Madonna was born on August 16, 1958.

August 17

1. Gabon was proclaimed an independent nation on August 17, 1960.
2. Davy Crockett, frontiersman, scout, and politician, was born on August 17, 1786.
3. Robert Fulton's steamboat, the *Clermont*, made a successful run up the Hudson River in New York on August 17, 1807.
4. Gold was discovered in the Klondike on this date in 1896.

August 18

1. On August 18, 1587, Virginia Dare became the first child born in America to English parents.
2. Meriwether Lewis, an explorer, was born on this date in 1774.
3. Baseball player Roberto Clemente was born on August 18, 1934.

August 19

1. Today is National Aviation Day. Orville Wright, inventor and airplane manufacturer, was born on August 19, 1871.
2. Ogden Nash, a writer of light verse, was born on August 19, 1902.
3. Bill Clinton, the 42nd president of the United States of America, was born on this day in 1946.

August 20

1. Benjamin Harrison, our twenty-third president, was "born into politics" on this date in 1833. His father was a congressman from Ohio, his grandfather was our ninth president, and his great-grandfather signed the Declaration of Independence.
2. Senegal was proclaimed an independent nation on August 20, 1960.
3. Naval hero Oliver H. Perry was born on this date in 1785.
4. In music history, Tchaikovsky's *1812 Overture* premiered on this day in 1882.

August 21

1. Hawaii was proclaimed our fiftieth state on August 21, 1959. It is made up of 132 islands, including the eight main islands.
2. The Lincoln-Douglas debates began on August 21, 1858.
3. On August 21, 1967, the U.S. Defense Department announced that two of its jets bound for North Vietnam had been shot down over the People's Republic of China.

August 22

1. The first local chapter of the American Red Cross was founded on August 22, 1881, by Clara Barton.
2. On August 22, 1989, Nolan Ryan became the first pitcher in major league baseball history to strike out 5,000 batters in a career.
3. On this day in 1902, Theodore Roosevelt became the first president to ride in an automobile.

August 23

1. Edgar Lee Masters, poet and biographer, was born on August 23, 1869.
2. On this day in 1927, Nicola Sacco and Bartolomeo Vanzetti were executed in Massachusetts for a crime that some felt the two did not commit.
3. On August 23, 1989, Victoria Brucker of San Pedro, California, became the first girl to play in a Little League World Series game.

August 24

1. The White House was burned by the British on August 24, 1814.
2. A volcano in Italy, Mt. Vesuvius, buried Pompeii under a thick blanket of ash after erupting on August 24, A.D. 79.
3. The waffle iron was patented on this day in 1869.
4. Baseball player Cal Ripken, Jr., who holds the record for most consecutive games

Answer Key (cont.)

played, was born on August 24, 1960.

August 25
1. Leonard Bernstein, composer and conductor, was born on this date in 1918.
2. Bret Harte, author and poet, was born on August 25, 1836.
3. Scottish actor Sean Connery was born on August 25, 1930. He is best known for playing James Bond in several movies.

August 26
1. Today is Women's Equality Day. The Nineteenth Amendment, granting women the right to vote, was adopted on August 26, 1920.
2. On August 26, 1903, the first automobile arrived in New York City after 52 days of travel across the U.S.
3. The first televised baseball game took place on this day in 1939. The teams that faced each other on that day were the Cincinnati Reds and the Brooklyn Dodgers.

August 27
1. The first radio message was sent from an airplane on August 27, 1910.
2. President Lyndon B. Johnson, our thirty-sixth president, was born on August 27, 1908.
3. The first oil well was drilled in the United States on August 27, 1859, at Titusville, Pennsylvania.

August 28
1. The first coal was mined in the U.S. on August 28, 1922.
2. The first United States commercial radio broadcast took place on August 28, 1922.
3. More than 200,000 Americans marched in Washington, D.C., on August 28, 1963, for civil rights. Among the leaders of the march were Jesse Jackson and the Reverend Dr. Martin Luther King, Jr.

August 29
1. On August 29, 1957, Congress passed the first Civil Rights Act since 1875.
2. Oliver Wendell Holmes was born on August 29, 1809. He wrote poetry and essays.
3. Pop star Michael Jackson was born on August 29, 1958, in Gary, Indiana.

August 30
1. Mary Wollstonecraft Shelley, author of *Frankenstein*, was born on August 30, 1797.
2. Guion Bluford, Jr., became the first African-American astronaut in space on this day in 1983.
3. An emergency communications link between Washington, D.C., and Moscow first went into operation on August 30, 1963.

August 31
1. Thomas Edison patented the kinetoscope on this day in 1887.
2. The Agricultural Hall of Fame was established on August 31, 1960.
3. The U.S. Department of Housing and Urban Development was established on August 31, 1965.

September 1
1. World War II began on September 1, 1939, when Germany attacked Poland.
2. On September 1, 1985, Dr. Robert Ballard discovered the *Titanic* sitting upright on the ocean bottom, 2.5 miles below the surface.
3. In 1998, a movie based on the sinking of the *Titanic* won an Academy Award for Best Picture. The movie, called *Titanic*, cost over 100 million dollars to make.

September 2
1. World War II ended on September 2, 1945, less than a month after the Allies dropped atomic bombs on Hiroshima and Nagasaki, Japan.
2. The United States Department of the Treasury was established on September 2, 1789.
3. Today in 1965, the musical group the Beatles released the song "Yesterday."

September 3
1. The signing of the Treaty of Paris officially ended the Revolutionary War on September 3, 1783.
2. Among other things, the Treaty of Paris established the United States' geographical borders.
3. *Viking II* landed on Mars to collect scientific data on this date in 1976.

September 4
1. Transcontinental television service began with the telecast of the Japanese Peace Conference. It took place on September 4, 1951.

Answer Key *(cont.)*

2. George Eastman received a patent for the first roll camera on this date in 1880.
3. It's Newspaper Carrier Day! In 1833 Barney Flaherty became the first newsboy in the United States.
4. Baseball player Mike Piazza was born on September 4, 1968.

September 5

1. The First Continental Congress met at Carpenters Hall on September 5, 1774.
2. Jesse James, a desperado, was born on this date in 1847.
3. The first Monday in September is Labor Day. It's observed to honor American workers. The first Labor Day parade was held on September 5, 1882.

September 6

1. President William McKinley was assassinated on September 6, 1901.
2. Jane Addams, a pioneer social worker and Nobel Peace Prize winner, was born today in 1860. She founded Hull House in Chicago in 1889. It was one of the first settlement houses in the United States.
3. Marquis de Lafayette, a French patriot, was born on this date in 1757.

September 7

1. Thomas Gregora, an eleven-year-old English boy, crawled ashore at Shakespeare Beach on September 7, 1860. He set a record as the youngest person to swim the English Channel.
2. Brazil became an independent nation on September 7, 1822.
3. Queen Elizabeth I of England was born on September 7, 1533.
4. Anna Mary Robertson Moses was born on September 7, 1860. She's known as Grandma Moses, and she started to paint in 1938 at age 78.

September 8

1. Today is International Literacy Day! To celebrate, read a book.
2. The Pledge of Allegiance was published on September 8, 1892.
3. St. Augustine, Florida, was founded on this date in 1565. It's the oldest city in the United States.
4. On 9/8/98, Mark McGwire of the St. Louis Cardinals hit his 62nd home run of the season, breaking the previous mark of 61 set in 1961. McGwire finished the year with an amazing 70 home runs!

September 9

1. California became the thirty-first state on September 9, 1850.
2. Edward E. Kleinschmidt, born on September 9, 1875, invented the teletype printer. His printer transmitted words through telephone wires.
3. Poet Aileen Fisher was born on September 9, 1906.
4. President Ford granted an unconditional pardon to former President Nixon on September 9, 1974.

September 10

1. Oliver H. Perry, a United States naval officer, won the Battle of Lake Erie on September 10, 1813.
2. Elias Howe patented the sewing machine on September 10, 1846.
3. *Guernica*, a famous painting by Pablo Picasso, arrived in Spain for the first time on September 10, 1981. Picasso, a Spanish artist, did not want this piece to be seen in Spain until the country was no longer ruled by Francisco Franco.

September 11

1. Alexander Hamilton was appointed the first Secretary of the Department of the Treasury on this day in 1789.
2. Henry Hudson sailed up the Hudson River on September 11, 1609.
3. William Sydney Porter was born on September 11, 1862. Using the pen name O. Henry, he wrote many short stories.

September 12

1. Hurricane Frederic struck the Gulf Coast on September 12, 1979. Its winds, which reached 130 mph, caused over $1.5 billion in damage.
2. Richard Hoe, inventor of the rotary press, was born on September 12, 1812.
3. The Soviet Union launched the first rocket to the moon on this date in 1959.

September 13

1. Milton S. Hershey, the candy bar maker, was born on this date in 1857.
2. Commodore John Barry, father of the United States Navy, died on this date in 1803.

Answer Key *(cont.)*

3. Walter Reed was born on September 13, 1851. This physician proved that a mosquito transmitted a deadly disease called yellow fever.
4. James Cleveland (Jesse) Owens was born on September 13, 1913. He is one of the most famous athletes in sports history. He won four gold medals in the 1936 Olympics in Berlin, Germany.

September 14
1. Theodore Roosevelt, our twenty-sixth president, took office on September 14, 1901, following the assassination of President McKinley.
2. Francis Scott Key wrote "The Star-Spangled Banner" on September 14, 1814. He became inspired while watching the British bombardment of Fort McHenry in the Chesapeake Bay.
3. The American Philatelic Society was formed on this date in 1886. Philatelists are people who collect stamps.
4. Hurricane Gilbert roared into the Gulf of Mexico on September 14, 1988. At times, its winds exceeded 200 miles an hour.

September 15
1. William Howard Taft was born on September 15, 1857, in Cincinnati, Ohio. He became our twenty-seventh president and was later appointed Chief Justice of the United States Supreme Court.
2. James Fenimore Cooper, author of *Tales of Frontier Life*, was born today in 1789.
3. Agatha Christie is remembered as an author of famous mysteries. She was born on September 15, 1890.

September 16
1. Mexico's Independence Day took place on September 16, 1810.
2. James J. Hill, a financier and railroad builder, was born on this date in 1838.
3. The *Mayflower* departed on September 16, 1620, from Plymouth, England. There were 102 passengers aboard heading for the New World.

September 17
1. Baron von Steuben, a German military officer who fought in the American Revolution, was born today in 1730.
2. The United States Constitution was signed on September 17, 1787, in Philadelphia, Pennsylvania. It went into effect nine months later on June 21, 1788. It was signed by 39 delegates and replaced the Articles of Confederation.
3. The first ten amendments to the U.S. Constitution are called the Bill of Rights.

September 18
1. The United States Air Force became a separate military service on this date in 1947.
2. President Washington laid the cornerstone of the Capitol building on September 18, 1793.
3. The Fugitive Slave Bill was passed on September 18, 1850. It required that escaped slaves be returned to their owners.
4. Samuel Johnson, an English author and dictionary maker, was born on September 18, 1709.

September 19
1. Our twentieth president, James Abram Garfield, died on this date in 1881. He was shot by Charles Guiteau. Garfield was president for fewer than four months.
2. President Washington's Farewell Address was published on September 19, 1796.
3. A cartoon starring Mickey Mouse was shown for the first time on September 19, 1928.

September 20
1. Ferdinand Magellan left Spain on September 20, 1519, to find a new route to the Spice Islands. One of his ships was the first to circle the globe.
2. Alexander the Great was born on September 20, 356 B.C.
3. In a highly publicized tennis match, female tennis player Billie Jean King beat male tennis player Bobby Riggs in three sets on this date in 1973.

September 21
1. Louis Joliet, a French fur trader and explorer, was born on September 21, 1645.
2. Today marks the beginning of autumn.

Answer Key (cont.)

3. On September 21, 1988, Dr. Lauro F. Cavazos became the first person of Hispanic descent to serve as a Cabinet member.

September 22
1. Michael Faraday, an England scientist and pioneer in electricity, was born on September 22, 1791.
2. The British put Nathan Hale to death as a spy on this date in 1776. He is remembered for saying, "I only regret that I have but one life to lose for my country."
3. Italo Marchiony applied for a patent for the ice-cream cone on September 22, 1903. It was issued on December 15, 1903.

September 23
1. Euripides, the last of the three most famous Greek dramatists of the ancient world, was born on September 23, 480 B.C.
2. Augustus Caesar, the first Roman emperor, was born on September 23, 63 B.C.
3. Captain John Paul Jones captured the *Serapis*, a British warship, on this date in 1779.
4. William McGuffey, compiler of *McGuffey's Eclectic Readers*, was born on September 23, 1800.
5. The planet Neptune was discovered on September 23, 1846.

September 24
1. On September 24, 1906, Devil's Tower, Wyoming, became the first national monument in the United States.
2. The United States Supreme Court was created on September 24, 1789.
3. John Marshall, a United States Supreme Court Chief Justice, was born on this date in 1755.
4. Jim Henson, creator of the Muppets, was born on September 24, 1936.

September 25
1. European Vasco Nuñez de Balboa sighted the Pacific Ocean on September 25, 1513. He saw it from the top of a mountain in what is now Panama.
2. Alfred Vail, who helped developed Morse code, was born on this date in 1807.
3. Christopher Columbus set sail on his second voyage to America on September 25, 1493.

4. Benjamin Harris published the first newspaper in America on this date in 1690.

September 26
1. Thomas Jefferson was appointed the first Secretary of State on September 26, 1789.
2. The Federal Trade Commission was established on September 26, 1914.
3. John Philip Sousa performed his first concert on this date in 1895. He's known as a march composer.
4. Today is Johnny Appleseed Day. John "Johnny Appleseed" Chapman was born on September 26, 1775.

September 27
1. Edwin Booth, a famous American actor, made his New York City debut on September 27, 1850. Fifteen years later, Edwin's brother John would make headlines of his own. What did John Booth do?
2. Samuel Adams, a hero of the American Revolution, was born on September 27, 1722.
3. Thomas Nast, an editorial cartoonist, was born on this date in 1840.
4. Hiram Rhode Revels was born on September 27, 1822. He was the first African-American senator. He took office on February 25, 1870.

September 28
1. On September 28, 1909, Al Capp was born. He was the cartoonist and creator of "Li'l Abner."
2. Today is Confucius' birthday. He was born in China nearly 2,500 years ago. He said, "What you do not wish for yourself, do not do to others."
3. President Millard Fillmore named Brigham Young the first governor of the territory of Utah on September 28, 1850.

September 29
1. The first telephone message was sent across the U.S. on September 29, 1915.
2. Enrico Fermi, a Nobel Prize winner in physics, was born on this date in 1901.
3. The bobbies of Scotland Yard made their first public appearance on September 29, 1829.

Answer Key *(cont.)*

September 30
1. Ether was first used as an anesthetic on September 30, 1846.
2. The first hydroelectric power station opened on this date in 1882.
3. The TV cartoon *The Flintstones* premiered on this day in 1960.

October 1
1. James Earl Carter, our thirty-ninth president, was born on October 1, 1924. The Mideast Peace Treaty was signed in March of 1979 during President Carter's administration.
2. The first game of the first World Series ever played took place on October 1, 1903.
3. The first Model T Ford was introduced on October 1, 1908.
4. Nigeria was proclaimed an independent nation on this date in 1960.

October 2
1. On October 2, 1872, Jules Verne introduced *Around the World in Eighty Days*.
2. Mohandas K. Gandhi, an Indian pacifist, was born on October 2, 1869.
3. The Wild and Scenic Rivers Act was passed on this date in 1968.
4. Robert H. Lawrence, the first African-American astronaut, was born today in 1935.
5. Charlie Brown and his friends were born on October 2, 1950.

October 3
1. On this day in 1863, President Abraham Lincoln declared Thanksgiving a national holiday.
2. Thurgood Marshall became the first African-American Supreme Court justice on October 3, 1967.
3. William Crawford Gorgas was born on this date in 1854. He developed the cure for yellow fever.
4. John Thurman patented the first vacuum cleaner on October 3, 1899.

October 4
1. Saint Francis of Assisi was born on October 4, 1181 or 1182. He and his followers formed the Franciscan Order of Monks.
2. President Rutherford B. Hayes, our nineteenth president, was born on this date in 1822.

3. On October 4, 1582, Pope Gregory XIII announced that the next day would not be October 5 but October 15. He changed the Julian calendar to the Gregorian calendar.

October 5
1. President Chester A. Arthur, our twenty-first president, was born on October 5, 1830.
2. President Harry S Truman made the first presidential address telecast from the White House on this date in 1947.
3. Robert Goddard was born on October 5, 1882. This "Father of the Space Age" was often ridiculed and ignored because he dreamed of rocket travel to other planets.

October 6
1. George Westinghouse, inventor and manufacturer, was born on October 6, 1846.
2. Thomas A. Edison showed the first movie in West Orange, New Jersey, on this date in 1889.
3. Explorer and author Thor Heyerdahl was born on this date in 1914. He believed Indians from South America might have settled the Polynesian Islands. In 1947 he sailed a balsa-wood raft from Peru to Polynesia to prove he might be right.

October 7
1. On this date in 1986, President Ronald Reagan signed a bill which made the rose the national flower of the United States.
2. James Whitcomb Riley, writer of *Little Orphan Annie*, was born on October 7, 1849.
3. On October 7, 1993, Toni Morrison became the first African-American woman to win the Nobel Prize for Literature.

October 8
1. Civil Rights leader Jesse L. Jackson was born on October 8, 1941.
2. The Great Chicago Fire began on October 8, 1871. This fire left 300 people dead and 90,000 without homes.
3. On this date in 1871, a forest fire at Peshtigo, Wisconsin, burned six counties and killed more than 1,100 people.

Answer Key *(cont.)*

4. On October 8, 1945, Paul Robeson was awarded the Spingarn Medal for distinguished achievement in theater and concert.

October 9

1. Uganda was proclaimed an independent nation on October 9, 1962.
2. The Fingerprint Society was founded on this date in 1915.
3. Today is Leif Ericson Day! This celebrates the discovery of North America about the year A.D. 1000 by Leif Ericson, a Norse explorer.
4. The Washington Monument was opened to the public on October 9, 1888. It is over 555 feet tall!

October 10

1. The United States Naval Academy opened at Annapolis on October 10, 1845.
2. Martina Navratilova, a skilled tennis player, was born in Czechoslovakia on October 10, 1956.
3. Vice President Spiro T. Agnew, who served under President Richard Nixon, resigned from office on October 10, 1973, due to charges of tax evasion.

October 11

1. Eleanor Roosevelt, wife of our thirty-second president, was born on October 11, 1884. For many years she was a delegate to the United Nations.
2. *Apollo 7*, the first manned Apollo mission, was successfully launched on October 11, 1968.
3. Today is General Casimir Pulaski Memorial Day. Pulaski, a hero of the Revolutionary War, died on this date in 1779.

October 12

1. Columbus sighted San Salvador Island in Central America on October 12, 1492.
2. Elmer A. Sperry, inventor of the gyrocompass, was born on this date in 1860.
3. On October 12, 1960, Soviet Premier Nikita Khrushchev made a famous speech in front of the United Nations Assembly. During the speech, Khrushchev pounded on a desk with a shoe to emphasize his point.

October 13

1. The White House cornerstone was laid on October 13, 1792.
2. Today is the birthday of the U.S. Navy. It's been in operation since 1775.
3. Football player Jerry Rice was born on October 13, 1962. Rice is generally considered to be the greatest wide receiver in professional football history.

October 14

1. Dwight David Eisenhower, our thirty-fourth president, was born on this date in 1890. "Ike" had a successful military career prior to his presidency.
2. William Penn, founder of the Pennsylvania colony, was born on October 14, 1644.
3. Chuck Yeager was the first human to break the sound barrier by flying the rocket-powered Bell X-1 airplane. He did it on this date in 1947.
4. On October 14, 1066, William the Conqueror and Edward fought for the English crown at the Battle of Hastings. William won.

October 15

1. On this date in 1966, President Lyndon Johnson signed a bill which created the U.S. Department of Transportation.
2. The TV show *I Love Lucy* premiered on October 15, 1951.
3. The first televised weather report took place on this date in 1953.

October 16

1. On October 16, 1859, John Brown and his followers seized the federal arsenal in Harpers Ferry, West Virginia. Brown, a white man who was executed for his actions, fought to abolish slavery.
2. Today is Dictionary Day! Noah Webster, writer of the first American dictionary, was born on October 16, 1758.
3. Benjamin O. Davis, Sr., became the first African-American general in the regular Army. He did so on October 16, 1940.
4. Today is National Bosses Day!

October 17

1. General Burgoyne surrendered at Saratoga on October 17, 1777.
2. Jupiter Hammon was born on October 17, 1711. He was the first African American to publish his own verse of poetry.

Answer Key *(cont.)*

3. Shortly after 5:00 P.M. on October 17, 1989, a large earthquake struck San Francisco, California, collapsing a busy freeway and disrupting a World Series game which was about to begin.

October 18

1. On this date in 1968, American Bob Beamon set the world long jump record at the Summer Olympics in Mexico City, Mexico.
2. The Mason-Dixon Line was completed on October 18, 1767.
3. On this date in 1867, the American flag was raised at Sitka in what is now known as Alaska. It had been purchased from Russia for two cents an acre.

October 19

1. It's Yorktown Day. In 1781 British General Lord Cornwallis and more than 7,000 English and Hessian soldiers surrendered to General George Washington to end the war between Britain and the Colonies.
2. President John Adams was born on this date in 1735.
3. Thomas A. Edison's first successful demonstration of the electric light happened on October 19, 1879.

October 20

1. Herbert Clark Hoover, our thirty-first president, died on October 20, 1964. His life could be characterized by calling him a humanitarian.
2. John Dewey, an educator, was born on October 20, 1859.
3. Harold Harris was the first to use a parachute after his plane became disabled. It happened on October 20, 1922.

October 21

1. The USS *Constitution*, or "Old Ironsides," was launched on October 21, 1797.
2. On October 21, 1520, Magellan entered the strait that bears his name.
3. Alfred Nobel was born on October 21, 1833. This Swedish inventor's will has provided funds for the annual Nobel prize since 1901.

October 22

1. The original New York Metropolitan Opera House opened on October 22, 1883.
2. Sam Houston was inaugurated as the first president of the Republic of Texas on October 22, 1836.
3. Franz Liszt was born on October 22, 1811. This nineteenth-century Hungarian gave his first piano concert at the age of nine.

October 23

1. This is the day when people in San Juan Capistrano, California, watch as the swallows leave for a winter home further south.
2. Talk show host Johnny Carson was born on October 23, 1925.
3. Blanche Scott became the first woman to fly solo in an airplane on this date in 1910.

October 24

1. Today is United Nations Day! The charter for the United Nations was signed today in 1945.
2. Sara Josepha Hale was born on October 24, 1788. We have her to thank for our celebration of Thanksgiving.
3. The first transcontinental telegram was sent on this date in 1861. It traveled from San Francisco, California, to New York City, New York.

October 25

1. The George Washington Bridge, between New York and New Jersey, was opened on October 25, 1931.
2. Pablo Picasso, one of the world's greatest painters, was born in Spain on October 25, 1881.
3. Richard Evelyn Byrd was born on October 25, 1888. He devoted his life to aviation and polar exploration.

October 26

1. On October 26, 1994, Beverly Harvard became the first African-American woman to be named chief of police. On that day, the city of Atlanta, Georgia, appointed her to the position.
2. The Erie Canal opened on October 26, 1825. It was the first major man-made waterway in the United States. It extended from Lake Erie to the Hudson River.
3. The New York Public Library opened its doors on October 26, 1911.

October 27

1. The New York subway opened on this date in 1904. It was the first underwater and underground rail system ever built.

Answer Key *(cont.)*

2. President Theodore Roosevelt was born on October 27, 1858. He was the first president to ride in a car, submerge in a submarine, and fly in an airplane.
3. The first "talking" motion picture was shown to the public at Warner's Theater in New York City on October 26, 1927. Al Jolson had his screen debut in *The Jazz Singer*.

October 28

1. The Statue of Liberty was dedicated by President Grover Cleveland on October 28, 1886. Some know it as Liberty Enlightening the World.
2. During the dedication ceremony for the Statue of Liberty, the first ticker-tape parade took place.
3. Dr. Jonas Salk was born on October 28, 1914. He is responsible for the polio vaccination.
4. Terrell Davis, born on October 28, 1972, was the MVP of Super Bowl XXXII, which took place on January 25, 1998. XXXII is the Roman numeral version of what number?

October 29

1. The stock market crashed on October 29, 1929. This day, known as Black Tuesday, signaled the beginning of the Great Depression.
2. Edmund Halley, an astronomer who discovered a comet which is visible from Earth every 76 years or so, was born on October 29, 1656. Look for Halley's Comet in the year 2062!
3. The first trucking service started on October 29, 1904. It hauled goods between Colorado City, Colorado, and Snyder, Texas.

October 30

1. John Adams, our second president, was born on October 30, 1735. His son, John Quincy Adams, was our sixth president.
2. On October 30, 1938, a live radio program presented a play based on the book *War of the Worlds*, which described the invasion of Earth by Martians. Persons who tuned into the program late thought it was a real news broadcast and began to panic.
3. Ethel Waters, an actress and vocalist, was born on October 30, 1900.

October 31

1. Nevada became the thirty-sixth state on October 31, 1864.
2. Juliette Gordon Low, founder of the Girl Scouts, was born on October 31, 1860.
3. Today is National Magic Day! Harry Houdini, the great escape artist, died on October 31, 1926.
4. Work on the massive sculpture on Mount Rushmore was completed on this day in 1941.

November 1

1. Election Day for the presidency is the first Tuesday after the first Monday in November. This takes place every four years.
2. The White House became the official residence of the United States' presidents on November 1, 1800. John and Abigail Adams moved in on this date.
3. The first issue of *Crisis* was published by editor W. E. B. Du Bois on November 1, 1910.

November 2

1. There were only twenty-seven states in the Union when our eleventh president, James Knox Polk, took office. He was born on this date in 1795.
2. November 2, 1865, is the birth date of Warren Gamaliel Harding. He was born in Corsica, Ohio, and was our twenty-ninth president.
3. North Dakota became the thirty-ninth state and South Dakota became the fortieth state on November 2, 1889.
4. Daniel Boone, the trailblazer of Kentucky, was born on this date in 1734.
5. Howard Hughes' *Spruce Goose*, a huge airplane made of plywood, made its first and only flight on November 2, 1947. It was the world's largest plane.

November 3

1. Today is Sandwich Day, honoring the Fourth Earl of Sandwich. He was born today in England in 1718, and he invented the sandwich.
2. The first automobile show opened in New York City at Madison Square Garden on November 3, 1900.

Answer Key (cont.)

3. Panama gained its independence from Colombia on November 3, 1903. Soon after, the United States was granted permission to begin construction on the Panama Canal.

November 4
1. Humorist Will Rogers was born on November 4, 1879.
2. The Erie Canal formally opened on November 4, 1825.
3. King Tut's tomb was discovered on November 4, 1922, by archeologist Howard Carter.
4. The United States Embassy personnel were taken hostage in Iran on November 4, 1979.

November 5
1. The first colonial post office was established in Boston, Massachusetts, on November 5, 1639.
2. The first transcontinental flight was completed on November 5, 1911.
3. Crossword puzzles were first published in book form on this date in 1924.
4. Shirley Chisholm became the first African-American woman to be elected to the House of Representatives. She was elected on November 5, 1958.

November 6
1. Today is Adolphe Sax's birthday! He was born on November 6, 1814. He is the inventor of a musical instrument. Can you guess which one?
2. John Philip Sousa, march king and inventor of a musical instrument, was born on November 6, 1854.
3. James Naismith, inventor of basketball, was born on November 6, 1861.
4. The first intercollegiate football game in the United States was played on November 6, 1869.

November 7
1. On November 7, 1811, General William Henry Harrison defeated Indian attackers at the Battle of Tippecanoe.
2. Lewis and Clark's expedition reached the Pacific Ocean on November 7, 1805.
3. The last spike was driven in the Canadian Pacific Railway on November 7, 1885.
4. Marie Curie was born today in 1867. She was a French physicist who worked with her husband to research radioactivity.

November 8
1. Montana became the forty-first state on November 8, 1889. Its capital is Helena.
2. The first circulating library was established by Ben Franklin in Philadelphia on November 8, 1731.
3. Margaret Mitchell, author of *Gone with the Wind*, was born on November 8, 1900.

November 9
1. The Holocaust began on November 9, 1938. Nazi storm troopers systematically burned synagogues, looted Jewish shops, and began an era of persecution for all Jews.
2. Benjamin Banneker was born on November 9, 1731. He was an engineer, inventor, mathematician, and gazetteer.
3. President Theodore Roosevelt sailed on a United States battleship for the Panama Canal Zone. He was the first president to leave the country while serving in office. He set sail on November 9, 1906.

November 10
1. Vincent van Gogh's *Irises* sold for $53.9 million dollars on this date in 1987, making it the most expensive painting ever.
2. The United States Marine Corps was founded on November 10, 1775.
3. On November 10, 1903, patent no. 743,801 was issued to Mary Anderson of Massachusetts for the windshield wiper.

November 11
1. Washington became the forty-second state on November 11, 1889.
2. Today is Veterans Day! We honor the men and women who served our country in the armed services.
3. Massachusetts passed the first compulsory school law on November 11, 1647.

November 12
1. Auguste Rodin, a sculptor, was born on November 12, 1840. His most famous sculpture is called *The Thinker*.
2. Suffragist Elizabeth Cady Scanton was born on November 12, 1815. What is a suffragist?
3. Ellis Island, a United States immigration station, closed on November 12, 1954. It had been used as a detention and deportation center since 1891.

Answer Key *(cont.)*

November 13

1. The Holland Tunnel opened in New York City on November 13, 1927.
2. The Holland Tunnel connects Canal Street in Manhattan, New York, to Jersey City, New Jersey. It consists of two tubes that are over 8,000 feet in length!
3. Scottish author Robert Louis Stevenson was born on November 13, 1850. He wrote *Treasure Island* (1883), *A Child's Garden of Verses* (1885), and several other classics.

November 14

1. Robert Fulton, inventor of the steamboat, was born on November 14, 1765, in Lancaster County, Pennsylvania.
2. Claude Monet, a French painter, was born on November 14, 1840. He is famous for painting the same scene at different times of the day or year.
3. On November 14, 1969, three U.S. astronauts survived a launch aboard *Apollo 12,* which saw them lose power temporarily. Power was restored, and the mission was completed successfully.

November 15

1. Poet David McCord was born in New York City on November 15, 1897.
2. The Articles of Confederation was approved by Congress on November 15, 1777.
3. Pikes Peak was discovered by Zebulon Pike on November 15, 1806.
4. Today is Shichi-Go-San! This Japanese children's festival is one of the most picturesque events of autumn. Parents thank the guardian spirits for the healthy growth of their children, and prayers are offered for their further development.

November 16

1. The first spacecraft to land on Venus, the Soviet Union's *Venera 3*, was launched on this date in 1965.
2. Oklahoma was admitted to the Union on November 16, 1907.
3. W. C. Handy was born on November 16, 1873. This American composer and bandleader was called "The Father of the Blues."

November 17

1. The Suez Canal opened on November 17, 1869.
2. Lewis and Clark reached the Pacific Ocean on November 17, 1805.
3. The infamous *Heidi* game took place on this day in 1968. On that day, the end of a televised football game was not seen by the viewing audience when the network decided to show the children's program, *Heidi,* instead. The team which had been losing ended up winning in an exciting game.

November 18

1. Mickey Mouse first appeared on the screen in *Steamboat Willie* on this date in 1929. It was shown at the Colony Theater in New York City. It was the first animated talking picture.
2. Standard time began in the United States on November 18, 1883.
3. Louis Daguerre, father of photography, was born today in 1789.
4. The Panama Canal Zone was created on November 18, 1903.

November 19

1. Abraham Lincoln delivered the Gettysburg Address on November 19, 1863. He delivered his speech in two minutes. How long is four score and seven years?
2. President James A. Garfield, our twentieth president, was born on November 19, 1831, in Orange, Ohio.
3. George Rogers Clark, a frontiersman, was born on November 19, 1752.

November 20

1. Robert F. Kennedy was born on November 20, 1925.
2. Robert F. Kennedy served as attorney general of the United States under his brother, John F. Kennedy, and was in the process of campaigning for the 1968 presidency when he was assassinated.
3. Chester Gould was born on November 20, 1900. This popular cartoon artist created the "Dick Tracy" comic strip. He drew and wrote it from its first appearance in 1931 until 1977.

November 21

1. North Carolina was the twelfth state to ratify the Constitution. It did so on November 21, 1789. It seceded on May 20,

Answer Key *(cont.)*

1861, and was readmitted in 1868.
2. Thomas A. Edison invented the phonograph on November 21, 1877.
3. The Mayflower Compact was signed on this date in 1620.
4. Baseball player Ken Griffey, Jr., was born on November 21, 1969. He and his father Ken Griffey, Sr., were the first father and son duo to hit home runs for the same team in the same game in major league baseball history.

November 22
1. Our thirty-fifth president, John Fitzgerald Kennedy, was assassinated on November 22, 1963. He was the youngest president (age 43) in our history. He was also the youngest to die while in office. He died at age 46.
2. French explorer Sieur de La Salle was born on November 22, 1643.
3. SOS was adopted as the international distress signal on November 22, 1906.
4. Scientists at Harvard University were the first to isolate the gene, the basic unit of heredity. They accomplished this feat on November 22, 1969.

November 23
1. Franklin Pierce was one of our youngest presidents. He became our fourteenth president at the age of 48. He was born on this date in 1804.
2. Henry McCarty was born on November 23, 1859. He was better known as "Billy the Kid."
3. The Female Medical Educational Society of Boston, Massachusetts, was founded on November 23, 1848.

November 24
1. Joseph F. Glidden received a patent for barbed wire on November 24, 1874.
2. President Zachary Taylor, our twelfth president, was born on November 24, 1784.
3. Carlo Lorenzini, author of *Pinocchio,* was born on this date in 1826.
4. On November 24, 1963, Lee Harvey Oswald, alleged assassin of President John F. Kennedy, was shot by nightclub owner Jack Ruby. This marked the first time a television audience viewed a murder as it

was happening.
5. Scott Joplin, a pianist and composer, was born on November 24, 1868.

November 25
1. On this day in 1963, President John F. Kennedy was buried in Arlington National Cemetery in Arlington, Virginia. Arlington National Cemetery, which surrounds the former home of General Robert E. Lee, is also the burial site of William Howard Taft.
2. Andrew Carnegie, steel magnate and patron of libraries, was born on November 25, 1835.
3. Baseball star Joe DiMaggio was born on this date in 1914.

November 26
1. The first street railway in the United States began on November 26, 1832.
2. Charles Schulz, creator of "Peanuts," was born on this date in 1922.
3. Sojourner Truth, the first African American to speak out against slavery, died on this date in 1883.
4. *Casablanca,* starring Humphrey Bogart and Ingrid Bergman, premiered on this day in 1942. On March 2, 1944, it won the Academy Award for Best Picture of the Year.

November 27
1. Thanksgiving Day is the last Thursday in November. This tradition started in 1621, a year after the Pilgrims landed in the New World.
2. Magellan entered the Pacific Ocean on November 27, 1520.
3. The Army War College was established on November 27, 1901.
4. Inventive guitarist Jimi Hendrix was born on November 27, 1942.

November 28
1. William Blake, the English poet, was born on November 28, 1757. "The Tiger" is one of his poems.
2. The first United States post office opened in New York City on November 28, 1785.
3. Richard Wright, the author of *Native Son*

Answer Key (cont.)

and *Black Boy*, died on this date in 1960.

November 29

1. Admiral Richard Byrd flew over the South Pole on November 29, 1929.
2. Louisa May Alcott, author of such classics as *Little Women*, was born on this date in 1832.
3. Bobby Darin's song "Mack the Knife" won the Grammy Award for best song on November 29, 1959.

November 30

1. Samuel Clemens was born on November 30, 1835. His pen name is Mark Twain.
2. Jonathan Swift, author of *Gulliver's Travels*, was born on this date in 1667.
3. Winston Churchill, an English political leader, was born on November 30, 1874.

December 1

1. On December 1, 1955, Rosa Parks was arrested for refusing to relinquish her seat to a white passenger on a bus in Montgomery, Alabama.
2. Woody Allen was born on December 1, 1935. He has written, directed, and starred in several famous films.
3. Hanukkah, also known as the Festival of Lights, lasts eight days. It falls at the end of November or sometime during the month of December.

December 2

1. The Monroe Doctrine was announced by President James Monroe on December 2, 1823. It stated that the United States' foreign policy would be to separate itself entirely from European influence.
2. The first reindeer in the U.S. was purchased from Russia. It arrived in Alaska on December 2, 1892.
3. The first permanent artificial heart was implanted on December 2, 1982.

December 3

1. Illinois became the twenty-first state on December 3, 1818.
2. Ellen Henrietta Richards, founder of the home economics movement, was born on December 3, 1842.
3. The first heart transplant, which was performed by Dr. Christian Barnard, took place in South Africa on December 3, 1967.

December 4

1. The first man-made satellite to orbit the planet Venus was the *Pioneer Venus 1*. It began its orbit on December 4, 1978.
2. *The Amsterdam News*, the largest weekly community newspaper in the United States, was founded on this date in 1909.
3. The first agricultural society of importance in the U.S. was founded on December 4, 1867. It was called the Grange.

December 5

1. Martin Van Buren, our eighth president, was born on December 5, 1782. Before becoming president, he was President Jackson's secretary of state and later, his vice president.
2. Walt Disney, producer of animated cartoons, was born on December 5, 1901.
3. The Montgomery Bus Boycott, led by Martin Luther King, Jr., began on this date in 1955.
4. The Twenty-first Amendment to the Constitution was ratified on this day in 1933. This amendment repealed prohibition.

December 6

1. Joyce Kilmer, a poet, was born on this date in 1886.
2. On December 6, 1933, a federal judge lifted a ban on the novel *Ulysses* by James Joyce. When a work of art is banned because of its content, that is called censorship.
3. It's St. Nicholas Day, a day which honors a fourth-century bishop from Partara, Turkey.

December 7

1. Delaware was the first state to ratify the United States Constitution. It did so on December 7, 1787.
2. President Franklin D. Roosevelt proclaimed that December 7, 1941, was a day that would "live in infamy." On that day, Japanese forces attacked Pearl Harbor in Hawaii. This event marked the official beginning of the United States' involvement in World War II.
3. The first concert of the Philharmonic Symphony Society of New York played on this date in 1842.

Answer Key *(cont.)*

December 8
1. The first greeting card, designed by John Calcott Horsley, was printed on December 8, 1843.
2. Eli Whitney, inventor of the cotton gin, was born on December 8, 1765.
3. On December 8, 1980, former Beatle John Lennon was shot and killed outside of his New York City hotel by Mark David Chapman.

December 9
1. Clarence Birdseye was born on December 9, 1886. On a trip to Labrador, he noticed that quickly frozen fish were fresh and flavorful when thawed. What food process do you think he started?
2. Tanzania was proclaimed an independent nation on this date in 1961.
3. Richard Wright's novel *Native Son* was published on December 9, 1940.

December 10
1. Swedish chemist Alfred Nobel, the inventor of dynamite, died on this date in 1896. Money from his estate funds prizes for achievements in peace, literature, chemistry, physics, and medicine.
2. Martin Luther King, Jr., was awarded the Nobel Peace Prize on this date in 1964.
3. Today is Human Rights Day! The UN General Assembly adopted the Universal Declaration of Human Rights. This was done on December 10, 1948.
4. Emily Dickinson, a poet, was born today in 1830.
5. Mississippi became the twentieth state on December 10, 1817. It seceded in 1861. It was readmitted in 1870.

December 11
1. The United Nations International Children's Emergency Fund (UNICEF) was founded on this day in 1946.
2. On December 11, 1901, Guglielmo Marconi sent the first Morse code radio signal across the Atlantic from England to Newfoundland.
3. Indiana was admitted to the Union on December 11, 1816. It became the nineteenth state.
4. Robert Koch, a German physician and bacteriologist, was born on this date in 1843.

December 12
1. Today is Poinsettia Day. Dr. J. R. Poinsett, who introduced the poinsettia to the United States from Mexico, died on this date in 1851.
2. Pennsylvania was the second state to ratify the Constitution. It did so on December 12, 1787.
3. Kenya was proclaimed an independent nation on December 12, 1963.
4. Washington, D.C., became the official capital of the United States on this date in 1800.

December 13
1. The Susan B. Anthony silver dollar was first coined on December 13, 1978. It was the first U.S. coin to honor a woman.
2. Sir Francis Drake started a voyage around the world on December 13, 1577.
3. The clip-on tie was first designed on this day in 1928.

December 14
1. On December 14, 1819, Alabama became the twenty-second state to be admitted into the Union. It seceded on January 11, 1861, and was readmitted in 1868.
2. On December 14, 1911, Roald Amundsen, a Norwegian explorer, became the first person to reach the South Pole.
3. John Mercer Langston was one of the first African Americans to be elected to public office. He was born on December 14, 1829.
4. Margaret Chase Smith was born on December 14, 1897. She was the first woman in the United States to serve in both the House of Representatives and the Senate.

December 15
1. The first ten amendments, the Bill of Rights, were added to our Constitution on December 15, 1791.
2. Sitting Bull, a Sioux Indian leader, died on this day in 1890.
3. On December 15, 1939, the movie *Gone with the Wind* premiered in Atlanta, Georgia.

December 16
1. Tea anyone? The Boston Tea Party took place on December 16, 1773.

Answer Key (cont.)

2. The Germans began the Battle of the Bulge on December 16, 1944, during World War II.

3. Composer Ludwig van Beethoven was born on December 16, 1770.

December 17

1. The first successful airplane flight took place on December 17, 1903. Today is Wright Brothers Day!

2. Peter Shaffer's *Amadeus*, a play about the life of composer Wolfgang Amadeus Mozart, opened in New York City on December 17, 1980. The play later was made into a movie which won the Academy Award for Best Motion Picture.

3. On December 17, 1933, the first National Football League (NFL) championship game was played. On that day, the Chicago Bears beat the New York Giants by a score of 23 to 21.

December 18

1. New Jersey became the third state to ratify the Constitution. It did so on December 18, 1787.

2. The Thirteenth Amendment to the U.S. Constitution, which ended slavery, was ratified on December 18, 1865.

3. Joseph Grimaldi has been called the greatest clown in history. He was born on December 18, 1778.

December 19

1. Walter Williams, the last living Civil War veteran, died on December 19, 1959. He was 117 years old.

2. The Continental Army encamped at Valley Forge, Pennsylvania, on December 19, 1777. General Washington was commander of the troops.

3. Anthropologist Richard Leakey was born today in 1944.

4. The U.S. satellite *Atlas* broadcast the first radio voice from space on December 19, 1958. It was a recorded Christmas greeting from President Dwight D. Eisenhower.

December 20

1. The Louisiana Purchase was made from France on December 20, 1803. The United States purchased one million square miles for about $20.00 per square mile.

2. By this day in 1967, over 474,000 U.S. troops had been sent to Vietnam.

3. On December 20, 1977, President Jimmy Carter signed legislation which increased the Social Security tax.

December 21

1. Today is the first day of winter.

2. Today is Forefather's Day! The Pilgrims landed at Plymouth Rock, Massachusetts, on December 21, 1620.

3. *Apollo 8*, carrying the first humans to orbit the moon, was launched on this date in 1968.

4. On December 21, 1956, the Supreme Court's decision ended the Montgomery Bus Boycott with the integration of Montgomery buses.

December 22

1. The Lincoln Tunnel opened on December 22, 1937. It linked New York to New Jersey.

2. Colo was born at the Columbus Zoo on December 22, 1956. She was the first gorilla born in captivity.

3. Radio City Music Hall, located in New York City's Rockefeller Center, opened on December 22, 1932.

December 23

1. On December 23, 1975, the Metric Conversion Act was adopted. It made the metric system America's basic system of measurement.

2. The U.S. Federal Reserve System was established on December 23, 1913.

3. On this date in 1987, a plane landed in California after a journey of 24,986 miles. The plane had taken off on December 14 and returned on this day after making a nonstop flight around the world without refueling.

December 24

1. Frontiersman, scout, and soldier Kit Carson was born on December 24, 1809.

2. General Dwight D. Eisenhower was named Supreme Commander of Allied Forces on December 24, 1943.

3. December 24th is Christmas Eve for those who celebrate Christmas. Certain Christmas traditions, such as decorating Christmas tree and mailing Christmas cards, did not become popular customs until the 1800s.

Answer Key *(cont.)*

December 25
1. Sir Isaac Newton was born on December 25, 1642.
2. Mikhail Gorbachev resigned as leader of the Soviet Union on December 25, 1991. The Soviet Union dissolved into independent countries soon after this event.
3. Clara Barton, founder of the American Red Cross, was born on December 25, 1821.

December 26
1. While British troops quartered in Philadelphia, George Washington led his army across the Delaware River to New Jersey on December 25, 1776. He took 1,400 Hessian soldiers by surprise early on December 26th.
2. Today is the first day of Kwanzaa (first fruit). This African-American family observance has been held since 1966. It's a recognition of African harvest festivals.
3. Baseball player Ozzie Smith was born on December 26, 1954. He is known for his incredible defense.

December 27
1. What do pasteurization, vaccination, and the rabies vaccine have in common? All were invented or developed by Louis Pasteur, a French biochemist. He was born on December 27, 1822.
2. Sir George Cayley was born on December 27, 1773. He is considered to be the father of aerodynamics.
3. *Apollo 8* returned to Earth on December 27, 1968. During its mission, *Apollo 8* orbited the moon ten times.

December 28
1. Woodrow Wilson, our twenty-eighth president, was born on December 28, 1856.
2. Iowa was admitted as the twenty-ninth state on December 28, 1846.
3. W. F. Semple received the first patent for chewing gum. He did so on December 28, 1869.

4. "A penny saved is a penny earned." Benjamin Franklin made that statement. He began publishing *Poor Richard's Almanac* on this date in 1732.

December 29
1. Texas was admitted as the twenty-eighth state on December 29, 1845. It seceded from the Union on January 28, 1861, and was readmitted in 1870.
2. President Andrew Johnson, our seventeenth president, was born on this date in 1808.
3. The first YMCA in the U.S. was founded on December 29, 1851.
4. Pablo Casals was born in Spain on December 29, 1876. He was a master cello player.

December 30
1. Rudyard Kipling, an English poet and writer of *Jungle Book*, was born on December 30, 1865.
2. The first freeway in California opened on December 30, 1940. It connected Los Angeles to Pasadena.
3. Golfer Tiger Woods was born on December 30, 1975.

December 31
1. Ellis Island opened on December 31, 1890, as a U.S. port of entry for immigrants.
2. Baseball great Roberto Clemente died in a plane crash on December 31, 1972, while flying supplies for earthquake relief to Nicaragua. He ended his career with exactly 3,000 hits.
3. Hulan Jack became borough president of Manhattan on December 31, 1953. He was the first African American to hold a major elective office in a major American city.
4. Happy New Year!

Resources

Books

Alexander, Rosemary. *Top Notch 2 Teacher Tips: Seasons and Holidays.* Scholastic, Inc., 1991.

Buckle Down on American Citizenship. Profiles Corporation, 1992.

Carruth, Gorton. *The Encyclopedia of American Facts & Dates* (Eighth Edition). Harper & Row Publishers, 1987.

Hopkins, Lee Bennet, and Misha Arenstein. *Do You Know What Day Tomorrow Is?* Scholastic, Inc., 1990.

Kremer, John. *Celebrate Today.* Prima Publishing, 1996.

Resnick, Abraham, Margaret Pavol, and Helen Pappas. *Every Day's a Holiday.* Fearon Teacher Aids, 1991.

Sebranek, Patrick, Verne Meyer, and Dave Kemper. *Write Source 2000: A Guide to Writing, Thinking, and Learning.* Houghton Mifflin, 1995.

Sullivan, George. *Mr. President: A Book of U.S. Presidents.* Dodd, Mead & Company, Inc., 1984.

We the People. Center for Civic Education, 1995.

The World Book Encyclopedia. World Book, Inc., 1993.

Web Sites

American History Resource List
http://www.execpc.com/~dboals/amer.html

Biography.com
http://www.biography.com/

HyperHistory Online
http://www.hyperhistory.com/online_n2/History_n2/a.html

Invention Dimension
http://web.mit.edu/invent/

Library of Congress
http://lcweb.loc.gov/

POTUS Presidents of the United States
http://www.ipl.org/ref/POTUS/

Yahoo's Directory of Artists
http://dir.yahoo.com/Arts/Artists/Masters/

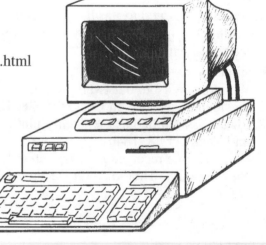